Photo by T. Charles Erickson

A scene from the Broadway production of "Buried Child." Set design by Robert Brill.

BURIED CHILD

CHILD

BY SAM SHEPARD

Revised Edition

★

★

DRAMATISTS
PLAY SERVICE
INC.

BURIED CHILD
Copyright © 1997 (Revised), Sam Shepard
Copyright © 1977, 1979, Sam Shepard

All Rights Reserved

SPECIAL NOTE

Rebirth }
Regeneration } life cycles

For Joe Chaikin

BURIED CHILD, the revised edition, was produced on Broadway by Frederick Zollo, Nicholas Paleologos, Jane Harmon, Nina Keneally, Gary Sinise, Edwin Schloss and Liz Oliver on April 30, 1996. The production transferred from the premiere production at Steppenwolf Theatre Company (Martha Lavey, Artistic Director; Michael Gennaro, Managing Director) in Chicago, Illinois, which opened on October 1, 1995. It was directed by Gary Sinise; the set design was by Robert Brill; the costume design was by Allison Reeds; the lighting design was by Kevin Rigdon; the sound design was by Rob Milburn; and the production stage manager was Laura Koch. The cast was as follows:

BRADLEY	Leo Burmester
DODGE	James Gammon
TILDEN	Terry Kinney
FATHER DEWIS	Jim Mohr
SHELLY	Kellie Overbey
HALIE	Lois Smith
VINCE	Jim True

BURIED CHILD was produced at Theater for the New City, in New York City, on October 19, 1978. It was directed by Robert Woodruff. The cast was as follows:

DODGE	Richard Hamilton
HALIE	Jacqueline Brookes
TILDEN	Tom Noonan
BRADLEY	Jay O. Sanders
SHELLY	Mary McDonnell
VINCE	Christopher McCann
FATHER DEWIS	Bill Wiley

BURIED CHILD received its premiere at the Magic Theatre, in San Francisco, California, on June 27, 1978. It was directed by Robert Woodruff. The cast was as follows:

DODGE	Joseph Gistirak
HALIE	Catherine Willis
TILDEN	Dennis Ludlow
BRADLEY	William M. Carr
SHELLY	Betsy Scott
VINCE	Barry Lane
FATHER DEWIS	Rj Frank

CHARACTERS

DODGE, in his seventies
HALIE, Dodge's wife; mid sixties
TILDEN, their oldest son
BRADLEY, their next oldest son, an amputee
VINCE, Tilden's son
SHELLY, Vince's girlfriend
FATHER DEWIS, a Protestant minister

BURIED CHILD

ACT ONE

Scene: day. Old wooden staircase down left with pale, frayed carpet laid down on the steps. The stairs lead offstage left up into the wings with no landing. Up right is an old, dark green sofa with the stuffing coming out in spots. Stage right of the sofa is an upright lamp with a faded yellow shade and a small night table with several small bottles of pills on it. Down right of the sofa, with the screen facing the sofa, is a large old-fashioned brown TV. A flickering blue light comes from the screen, but no image, no sound. In the dark, the light of the lamp and the TV slowly brighten in the black space. The space behind the sofa, upstage, is a large, screened-in porch with a board floor. A solid interior door to stage right of the sofa, leads from the porch to the outside. Beyond that are the shapes of dark elm trees.

Gradually the form of Dodge is made out, sitting on the couch, facing the TV, the blue light flickering on his face. He wears a well-worn T-shirt, suspenders, khaki work pants, and brown slippers. He's covered himself in an old brown blanket. He's very thin and sickly looking, in his late seventies. He just stares at the TV. More light fills the stage softly. The sound of light rain. Dodge slowly tilts his head back and stares at the ceiling for a while, listening to the rain. He lowers his head again and stares at the TV. He starts to cough slowly and softly. The coughing gradually builds. He holds one hand to his mouth and tries to stifle it. The coughing gets louder, then suddenly stops when he hears the sound of his wife's voice coming from the top of the staircase.

HALIE'S VOICE. Dodge? *(Dodge just stares at the TV. Long pause. He stifles two short coughs.)* Dodge! You want a pill, Dodge? *(He doesn't answer. Takes a bottle out from under cushion of sofa and takes a long swig. Puts the bottle back, stares at TV, pulls blanket up around his neck.)* You know what it is, don't you? It's the rain! Weather. That's it. Every time. Every time you get like this, it's the rain. No sooner does the rain start than you start. *(Pause)* Dodge? *(He makes no reply. Pulls a pack of cigarettes out from his sweater and lights one. Stares at TV. Pause.)* You should see it coming down up here. Just coming down in sheets. Blue sheets. The bridge is pretty near flooded. What's it like down there? Dodge? *(Dodge turns his head back over his left shoulder and takes a look out through the porch. He turns back to the TV.)*

DODGE. *(To himself.)* Catastrophic.

HALIE'S VOICE. What? What'd you say, Dodge?

DODGE. *(Louder.)* It looks like rain to me! Plain old rain!

HALIE'S VOICE. Rain? Of course it's rain! Are you having a seizure or something! Dodge? *(Pause.)* I'm coming down there in about five minutes if you don't answer me!

DODGE. Don't come down.

HALIE'S VOICE. What!

DODGE. *(Louder.)* Don't come down! *(He has another coughing attack. Stops.)*

HALIE'S VOICE. You should take a pill for that! I don't see why you just don't take a pill. Be done with it once and for all. Put a stop to it. *(He takes bottle out again. Another swig. Returns bottle.)* It's not Christian, but it works. It's not necessarily Christian, that is. A pill. We don't know. We're not in a position to answer something like that. There's some things the ministers can't even answer. I, personally, can't see anything wrong with it. A pill. Pain is pain. Pure and simple. Suffering is a different matter. That's entirely different. A pill seems as good an answer as any. Dodge? *(Pause.)* Dodge, are you watching baseball?

DODGE. No.

HALIE'S VOICE. What?

DODGE. *(Louder.)* No! I'm *not* watching baseball.

HALIE'S VOICE. What're you watching? You shouldn't be

8

watching anything that'll get you excited!

DODGE.   Nothing gets me excited.

HALIE'S VOICE.   No horse racing!

DODGE.   They don't race here on Sundays.

HALIE'S VOICE.   What?

DODGE.   *(Louder.)* They don't race on Sundays!

HALIE'S VOICE.   Well they shouldn't race on Sundays. The Sabbath.

DODGE.   Well they don't! Not here anyway. The boondocks.

HALIE'S VOICE.   Good. I'm amazed they still have that kind of legislation. Some semblance of morality. That's amazing.

DODGE.   Yeah, it's amazing.

HALIE'S VOICE.   What?

DODGE.   *(Louder.)* It *is* amazing!

HALIE'S VOICE.   It is. It truly is. I would've thought these days they'd be racing on Christmas even. A big flashing Christmas tree right down at the finish line.

DODGE.   *(Shakes his head.)* No. Not yet.

HALIE'S VOICE.   They used to race on New Year's! I remember that.

DODGE.   They never raced on New Year's!

HALIE'S VOICE.   Sometimes they did.

DODGE.   They never did!

HALIE'S VOICE.   Before we were married they did!

DODGE.   "Before we were married." *(Dodge waves his hand in disgust at the staircase. Leans back in sofa. Stares at TV.)*

HALIE'S VOICE.   I went once. With a man. On New Year's.

DODGE.   *(Mimicking her.)* Oh, a "man."

HALIE'S VOICE.   What?

DODGE.   Nothing!

HALIE'S VOICE.   A wonderful man. A breeder.

DODGE.   A what?

HALIE'S VOICE.   A breeder! A horse breeder! Thoroughbreds.

DODGE.   Oh, thoroughbreds. Wonderful. You betcha. A breeder-man.

HALIE'S VOICE.   That's right. He knew everything there was to know.

DODGE. I bet he taught you a thing or two huh? Gave you a good turn around the old stable!

HALIE'S VOICE. Knew everything there was to know about horses. We won bookoos of money that day.

DODGE. What?

HALIE'S VOICE. Money! We won every race I think.

DODGE. Bookoos?

HALIE'S VOICE. Every single race.

DODGE. Bookoos of money?

HALIE'S VOICE. It was one of those kind of days.

DODGE. New Year's!

HALIE'S VOICE. Yes! It might've been Florida. Or California! One of those two.

DODGE. Can I take my pick?

HALIE'S VOICE. It was Florida!

DODGE. Aha!

HALIE'S VOICE. Wonderful! Absolutely wonderful! The sun was just gleaming. Flamingos. Bougainvilleas. Palm trees.

DODGE. *(To himself, mimicking her.)* Flamingos. Bougainvilleas.

HALIE'S VOICE. Everything was dancing with life! Colors. There were all kinds of people from everywhere. Everyone was dressed to the nines. Not like today. Not like they dress today. People had a sense of style.

DODGE. When was this anyway?

HALIE'S VOICE. This was long before I knew you.

DODGE. Must've been.

HALIE'S VOICE. Long before. I was escorted.

DODGE. To Florida?

HALIE'S VOICE. Yes. Or it might've been California. I'm not sure which.

DODGE. All that way you were escorted?

HALIE'S VOICE. Yes.

DODGE. And he never laid a finger on you I suppose? This gentleman breeder-man. *(Long silence.)* Halie? Are we still in the land of the living? *(No answer. Long pause.)*

HALIE'S VOICE. Are you going out today?

DODGE. *(Gesturing toward rain.)* In this?

HALIE'S VOICE.   I'm just asking a simple question.

DODGE.   I rarely go out in the bright sunshine, why would I go out in this?

HALIE'S VOICE.   I'm just asking because I'm not doing any shopping today. And if you need anything you should ask Tilden.

DODGE.   Tilden's not here!

HALIE'S VOICE.   He's in the kitchen. *(Dodge looks toward L., then back toward TV.)*

DODGE.   All right.

HALIE'S VOICE.   What?

DODGE.   *(Louder.)* All right! I'll ask Tilden!

HALIE'S VOICE.   Don't scream. It'll only get your coughing started.

DODGE.   Scream? Men don't scream.

HALIE'S VOICE.   Just tell Tilden what you want and he'll get it. *(Pause.)* Bradley should be over later.

DODGE.   Bradley?

HALIE'S VOICE.   Yes. To cut your hair.

DODGE.   My hair? I don't need my hair cut! I haven't hardly got any hair left!

HALIE'S VOICE.   It won't hurt!

DODGE.   I don't need it!

HALIE'S VOICE.   It's been more than two weeks Dodge.

DODGE.   I don't need it! And I never did need it!

HALIE'S VOICE.   I have to meet Father Dewis for lunch.

DODGE.   You tell Bradley that if he shows up here with those clippers, I'll separate him from his manhood!

HALIE'S VOICE.   I won't be very late. No later than four at the very latest.

DODGE.   You tell him! Last time he left me near bald! And I wasn't even awake!

HALIE'S VOICE.   That's not my fault!

DODGE.   You put him up to it!

HALIE'S VOICE.   I never did!

DODGE.   You did too! You had some fancy, idiot house social planned! Time to dress up the corpse for company! Lower the ears a little! Put up a little front! Surprised you didn't tape

11

a pipe to my mouth while you were at it! That woulda looked nice! Huh? A pipe? Maybe a bowler hat! Maybe a copy of the *Wall Street Journal* casually placed on my lap! A fat labrador retriever at my feet.

HALIE'S VOICE.   You always imagine the worst things of people!

DODGE.   That's the least of the worst!

HALIE'S VOICE.   I don't need to hear it! All day long I hear things like that and I don't need to hear more.

DODGE.   You better tell him!

HALIE'S VOICE.   You tell him yourself! He's your own son. You should be able to talk to your own son.

DODGE.   Not while I'm sleeping! He cut my hair while I was sleeping!

HALIE'S VOICE.   Well he won't do it again.

DODGE.   There's no guarantee. He's a snake, that one.

HALIE'S VOICE.   I promise he won't do it without your consent.

DODGE.   *(After pause.)* There's no reason for him to even come over here.

HALIE'S VOICE.   He feels responsible.

DODGE.   For my hair?

HALIE'S VOICE.   For your appearance.

DODGE.   My appearance is out of his domain! It's even out of mine! In fact, it's disappeared! I'm an invisible man!

HALIE'S VOICE.   Don't be ridiculous.

DODGE.   He better not try it. That's all I've got to say.

HALIE'S VOICE.   Tilden will watch out for you.

DODGE.   Tilden won't protect me from Bradley!

HALIE'S VOICE.   Tilden's the oldest. He'll protect you.

DODGE.   Tilden can't even protect himself!

HALIE'S VOICE.   Not so loud! He'll hear you. He's right in the kitchen.

DODGE.   *(Yelling off L.)* Tilden!

HALIE'S VOICE.   Dodge, what are you trying to do?

DODGE.   *(Yelling off L.)* Tilden, get your ass in here!

HALIE'S VOICE.   Why do you enjoy stirring things up?

DODGE.   I don't enjoy anything!

HALIE'S VOICE. That's a terrible thing to say.

DODGE. Tilden!

HALIE'S VOICE. That's the kind of statement that leads people right to an early grave.

DODGE. Tilden!

HALIE'S VOICE. It's no wonder people have turned their backs on Jesus!

DODGE. TILDEN!!

HALIE'S VOICE. It's no wonder the messengers of God's word are shouting louder now than ever before. Screaming to the four winds.

DODGE. TILDEN!!!! *(Dodge goes into a violent, spasmodic coughing attack as Tilden enters from L., his arms loaded with fresh ears of corn. Tilden is Dodge's oldest son, late forties, wears heavy construction boots covered with mud, dark green work pants, a plaid shirt and a faded brown windbreaker. He has a butch haircut, wet from the rain. Something about him is profoundly burned-out and displaced. He stops C. with the ears of corn in his arms and just stares at Dodge until he slowly finishes his coughing attack. Dodge looks up at him slowly. Dodge stares at the corn. Long pause as they watch each other.)*

HALIE'S VOICE. Dodge, if you don't take that pill nobody's going to force you. Least of all me. There's no honor in self-destruction. No honor at all. *(The two men ignore the voice.)*

DODGE. *(To Tilden.)* Where'd you get that?

TILDEN. Picked it.

DODGE. You picked all that? *(Tilden nods.)* You expecting company?

TILDEN. No.

DODGE. Where'd you pick it from?

TILDEN. Right out back.

DODGE. Out back where!

TILDEN. Right out in back.

DODGE. There's nothing out there — in back.

TILDEN. There's corn.

DODGE. There hasn't been corn out there since about nineteen thirty-five! That's the last time I planted corn out there!

TILDEN. It's out there now.

DODGE. *(Yelling at stairs.)* Halie!

13

HALIE'S VOICE. Yes dear! Have you come to your senses?

DODGE. Tilden's brought a whole bunch of sweet corn in here! There's no corn out back is there?

TILDEN. *(To himself.)* There's tons of corn.

HALIE'S VOICE. Not that I know of!

DODGE. That's what I thought.

HALIE'S VOICE. Not since about nineteen thirty-five!

DODGE. *(To Tilden.)* That's right. Nineteen thirty-five. That was the last of it.

TILDEN. It's out there now.

DODGE. You go and take that corn back to wherever you got it from!

TILDEN. *(After pause, staring at Dodge.)* It's picked. I picked it all in the rain. Once it's picked you can't put it back.

DODGE. I haven't had trouble with the neighbors here for fifty-seven years. I don't even know who the neighbors are! And I don't wanna know! Now go put that corn back where it came from! *(Tilden stares at Dodge then walks slowly over to him and dumps all the corn on Dodge's lap and steps back. Dodge stares at the corn then back to Tilden. Long pause.)* Are you having trouble here, Tilden? Are you in some kind of trouble again?

TILDEN. I'm not in any trouble.

DODGE. You can tell me if you are. I'm still your father.

TILDEN. I know that.

DODGE. I know you had a little trouble back there in New Mexico. That's why you came out here. Isn't that the reason you came back?

TILDEN. I never had any trouble.

DODGE. Tilden, your mother told me all about it.

TILDEN. What'd she tell you? *(Tilden pulls some chewing tobacco out of his jacket and bites off a plug.)*

DODGE. I don't have to repeat what she told me! She told me all about it!

TILDEN. Can I bring my chair in from the kitchen?

DODGE. What?

TILDEN. Can I bring in my chair from the kitchen?

DODGE. That's not a chair it's a stool. Milking stool.

TILDEN. Can I bring it in here?

DODGE.   Sure. Bring it in here. Bring it on in here. Just don't call it a chair when it's a stool. *(Tilden exits L. Dodge pushes all the corn off of his lap onto the floor. He pulls the blanket off angrily and tosses it at one end of the sofa, pulls out the bottle and takes another swig. Tilden enters again from L. with a milking stool and a pail. Dodge hides the bottle quickly under the cushion before Tilden sees it. Tilden sets the stool down by the sofa, sits on it, puts the pail in front of him on the floor. Tilden starts picking up the ears of corn one at a time and husking them. He throws the husks and silk in the center of the stage and drops the ears into the pail each time he cleans one. He repeats this process as they talk. After pause.)* Pretty good-lookin' corn.

TILDEN.   Golden.

DODGE.   Hybrid?

TILDEN.   What?

DODGE.   Some kinda fancy hybrid?

TILDEN.   You planted it. I don't know what it is. *(Pause.)*

DODGE.   I never planted it. *(Pause.)* Tilden, look, you can't stay here forever. You know that, don't you? *(Tilden spits in spittoon.)*

TILDEN.   I'm not.

DODGE.   I know you're not. I'm not worried about that. That's not the reason I brought it up.

TILDEN.   What's the reason?

DODGE.   The reason is I'm wondering what you're gonna do with yourself.

TILDEN.   You're not worried about me, are you?

DODGE.   I'm not worried about you. No. I'm just wondering.

TILDEN.   You weren't worried about me when I wasn't here. When I was in New Mexico.

DODGE.   No, I wasn't worried about you then either.

TILDEN.   You shoulda worried about me then.

DODGE.   Why's that? You didn't do anything down there, did you? Nothin' serious.

TILDEN.   I didn't do anything. No.

DODGE.   Then why should I have worried about you?

TILDEN.   Because I was by myself.

15

DODGE. By yourself?

TILDEN. Yeah. I was by myself more than I've ever been before.

DODGE. Why was that? *(Pause.)*

TILDEN. Could I have some of that whiskey you've got?

DODGE. What whiskey? I haven't got any whiskey.

TILDEN. You've got some under the sofa.

DODGE. I haven't got anything under the sofa! Now mind your own damn business! Judas Priest, you come into the house outa the middle of nowhere, haven't heard or seen you in twenty-some years and suddenly you're making accusations.

TILDEN. I'm not making accusations.

DODGE. You're accusing me of hoarding whiskey under the sofa!

TILDEN. I'm not accusing you.

DODGE. You just got through telling me that I had whiskey under the sofa!

HALIE'S VOICE. Dodge?

DODGE. *(To Tilden.)* Now she knows about it!

TILDEN. She doesn't know about it.

DODGE. She knows!

HALIE'S VOICE. Dodge, are you talking to yourself down there?

DODGE. I'm talking to Tilden!

HALIE'S VOICE. Tilden's down there?

DODGE. He's right here!

HALIE'S VOICE. What?

DODGE. *(Louder.)* He's right here!

HALIE'S VOICE. What's he doing?

DODGE. *(To Tilden.)* Don't answer her.

TILDEN. *(To Dodge.)* I'm not doing anything wrong.

DODGE. *(To Tilden.)* I know you're not.

HALIE'S VOICE. What's he doing down there!

DODGE. *(To Tilden.)* Don't answer. Whatever you do, don't answer her.

TILDEN. I'm not.

HALIE'S VOICE. Dodge! *(The men sit in silence. Dodge lights a cigarette. Tilden keeps husking corn, spits tobacco now and then*

16

in spittoon.) Dodge! He's not drinking anything, is he? You see to it that he doesn't drink anything! You've gotta watch out for him. It's our responsibility. He can't look after himself anymore, so we have to do it. Nobody else will do it. We can't just send him away somewhere. If we had lots of money we could send him away. But we don't. We never will. That's why we have to stay healthy. You and me. Nobody's going to look after us. Bradley can't look after us. Bradley can hardly look after himself. I was always hoping that Tilden would look out for Bradley when they got older. After Bradley lost his leg. Tilden's the oldest. I always thought he'd be the one to take responsibility. I had no idea in the world that Tilden would be so much trouble. Who would've dreamed. Tilden was an All-American, don't forget. Don't forget that. Fullback. Or quarterback. I forget which.

TILDEN. *(To himself.)* Halfback.

DODGE. Don't make a peep. Just let her babble. *(Tilden goes on husking.)*

HALIE'S VOICE. Then when Tilden turned out to be so much trouble, I put all my hopes on Ansel. Of course Ansel wasn't as handsome, but he was smart. He was the smartest probably. I think he probably was. Smarter than Bradley, that's for sure. Didn't go and chop his leg off with a chain saw. Smart enough not to go and do that. I think he was smarter than Tilden too. Especially after Tilden got in all that trouble. Doesn't take brains to go to jail. Anybody knows that. Course then when Ansel passed that left us all alone. Same as being alone. No different. Same as if they'd all died. He was the smartest. He could've earned lots of money. Lots and lots of money.

DODGE. Bookoos. *(Halie enters slowly from the top of the staircase as she continues talking. Just her feet are seen at first as she makes her way down the stairs a step at a time. She appears dressed completely in black, as though in mourning. Black handbag, hat with a veil, and pulling on elbow-length black gloves. She is about sixty-five with pure white hair. She remains absorbed in what she's saying as she descends the stairs and doesn't really notice the two men who continue sitting there as they were before she came down, smoking and husking.)*

HALIE.   He would've took care of us, too. He would've seen to it that we were repaid. He was like that. He was a hero. Don't forget that. A genuine hero. Brave. Strong. And very intelligent.

TILDEN.   Ansel was a hero?

HALIE.   Ansel could've been a great man. One of the greatest. I only regret that he didn't die in action. It's not fitting for a man like that to die in a motel room. A soldier. He could've won a medal. He could've been decorated for valor. I've talked to Father Dewis about putting up a plaque for Ansel. He thinks it's a good idea. He agrees. He knew Ansel when he used to play basketball. Went to every game. Ansel was his favorite player. He even recommended to the City Council that they put up a statue of Ansel. A big, tall statue with a basketball in one hand and a rifle in the other. That's how much he thinks of Ansel.

TILDEN.   Ansel was a hero? *(Dodge kicks him. Halie reaches the stage and begins to wander around, still absorbed in pulling on her gloves, brushing lint off her dress and continuously talking to herself as the men just sit.)*

HALIE.   Of course, he'd still be alive today if he hadn't married into the Catholics. The Mob. How in the world he never opened his eyes to that is beyond me. Just beyond me. Everyone around him could see the truth. Even Tilden. Tilden told him time and again. Catholic women are the Devil incarnate. He wouldn't listen.

TILDEN.   I don't remember that. I must've been gone somewhere.

HALIE.   He was blind with love. Blind. I knew. Everyone knew. The wedding was more like a funeral. You remember? All those Italians. All that horrible black, greasy hair. The rancid smell of cheap cologne. I think even the priest was wearing a pistol. When he gave her the ring I knew he was a dead man. I knew it. As soon as he gave her the ring. But then it was the honeymoon that killed him. The honeymoon. I knew he'd never come back from the honeymoon. *(She stops abruptly and stares at the corn husks. She looks around the space as though just waking up. She turns hard and looks hard at Tilden and Dodge who continue sitting calmly. She looks again at the corn husks. Pointing to the husks.)* What's this in my house! *(Kicks husks.)* What's all this mess? *(Tilden stops husking and stares at her. To Dodge.)* And you encourage him! *(Dodge pulls blanket over himself again.)*

DODGE.   You're going out in the rain for a little soiree.

HALIE.   It's not raining now, is it. *(Tilden starts husking again.)*

DODGE.   Not in Florida it's not.

HALIE.   We're not in Florida!

DODGE.   It's not raining at the racetrack.

HALIE.   Have you been taking those pills? Those pills always make you talk crazy. Tilden, has he been taking those pills? Those teeny little blue pills.

TILDEN.   He hasn't took anything.

HALIE.   *(To Dodge.)* What've you been taking?

DODGE.   It's not raining in California or Florida or at the racetrack. Only in Illinois. This is the only place it's raining. All over the rest of the world it's bright golden sunshine. *(Halie goes to the night table next to the sofa and checks the bottle of pills.)*

HALIE.   Which ones did you take? Tilden, you must've seen him take something.

TILDEN.   He never took a thing.

HALIE.   Then why's he talking crazy?

DODGE.   Crazy. Crazy, crazy, crazy.

TILDEN.   I've been here the whole time.

HALIE.   Then you've both been taking something!

TILDEN.   I've just been husking the corn.

HALIE.   Where'd you get that corn anyway? Why is the house suddenly full of corn?

DODGE.   Bumper crop! Unexplainable.

HALIE.   *(Moving C.)* We haven't had corn here for over thirty years.

TILDEN.   The whole back lot's full of corn. Far as the eye can see. Like an ocean.

DODGE.   *(To Halie.)* Things keep happening while you're upstairs, ya know. The world doesn't stop just because you're upstairs. Corn keeps growing. Rain keeps raining.

HALIE.   I'm not unaware of the world around me! Thank you very much. It so happens that I have an overall view from the upstairs. A panorama. The backyard's in plain view of my window. And there's no corn to speak of. Absolutely none!

DODGE.   Tilden wouldn't lie. If he says there's corn, there's corn.

HALIE.   What's the meaning of this corn Tilden!

TILDEN.   It's a mystery to me. I was out in back there. And the rain was coming down. And I didn't feel like coming back inside. I didn't feel the cold so much. I didn't mind the wet. So I was just walking. I was muddy but I didn't mind the mud so much. And I looked up. And I saw this stand of corn. In fact I was standing in it. Surrounded. It was over my head.

HALIE.   There isn't any corn outside Tilden! There's no corn! It's not the season for corn. Now, you must've either stolen this corn or you bought it.

DODGE.   He doesn't have a red cent to his name. He's totally dependent.

HALIE.   *(To Tilden.)* So you stole it!

TILDEN.   I didn't steal it. I don't want to get kicked out of Illinois. I was kicked out of New Mexico and I don't want to get kicked out of Illinois.

HALIE.   You're going to get kicked out of this house, Tilden, if you don't tell me where you got that corn! *(Tilden starts crying softly to himself but keeps husking corn. Pause.)*

DODGE.   *(To Halie.)* Why'd you have to tell him that? Who cares where he got the corn? Why'd you have to go and threaten him with expulsion?

HALIE.   *(To Dodge.)* It's your fault you know! You're the one that's behind all of this! I suppose you thought it'd be funny! Some joke! Cover the house with corn husks. You better get this cleaned up before Bradley sees it.

DODGE.   Bradley's not getting in the front door!

HALIE.   *(Kicking husks, striding back and forth.)* Bradley's going to be very upset when he sees this. He doesn't like to see the house in disarray. He can't stand it when one thing is out of place. The slightest thing. You know how he gets.

DODGE.   Bradley doesn't even live here!

HALIE.   It's his home as much as ours. He was born in this house!

DODGE.   He was born in a hog wallow.

HALIE.   Don't you say that! Don't you ever say that!

DODGE.   He was born in a goddamn hog wallow! That's where he was born and that's where he belongs! He doesn't belong in this house! *(Halie stops.)*

HALIE.   I don't know what's come over you, Dodge. I don't know what in the world's come over you. You've become an evil, spiteful, vengeful man. You used to be a good man.

DODGE.   Six of one, a half-dozen of another.

HALIE.   You sit here day and night, festering away! Decomposing! Smelling up the house with your putrid body! Hacking your head off 'til all hours of the morning! Thinking up mean, evil, stupid things to say about your own flesh and blood!

DODGE.   He's not my flesh and blood! My flesh and blood's out there in the backyard! *(They freeze. Long pause. The men stare at her.)*

HALIE.   *(Quietly.)* That's enough, Dodge. That's quite enough. You've become confused. I'm going out now. I'm going to have lunch with Father Dewis. I'm going to ask him about a monument for Ansel. A statue. At least a plaque.

DODGE.   That oughta heal things up. A statue. *(She crosses to the door up R. She stops.)*

HALIE.   If you need anything, ask Tilden. He's the oldest. I've left some money on the kitchen table.

DODGE.   I don't need a thing.

HALIE.   No, I suppose not. *(She opens the door and looks out through porch.)* Still raining. I love the smell just after it stops. The ground. It's like the ground is breathing. I won't be too late. *(She goes out door and closes it. She's still visible on the porch as she crosses toward L. screen door. She stops in the middle of the porch, speaks to Dodge but doesn't turn to him.)* Dodge, tell Tilden not to go out in the back lot anymore. I don't want him back there in the rain. He's got no business out there.

DODGE.   You tell him yourself. He's sitting right here.

HALIE.   He never listens to me Dodge. He's never listened

21

to me in the past.

DODGE. I'll tell him.

HALIE. We have to watch him just like we used to now. Just like we always have. He's still a child.

DODGE. I'll watch him.

HALIE. Good. We don't want to lose him. I couldn't take another loss. Not at this late date. *(She crosses to screen door, L., takes an umbrella off a hook and goes out the door. The door slams behind her. Long pause. Tilden husks corn, stares at pail. Dodge lights a cigarette, stares at TV.)*

TILDEN. *(Still husking.)* You shouldn't a told her that.

DODGE. *(Staring at TV.)* What?

TILDEN. What you told her. You know.

DODGE. What do you know about it?

TILDEN. I know. I know all about it. We all know.

DODGE. So what difference does it make? Everybody knows, everybody's forgot.

TILDEN. She hasn't forgot.

DODGE. She should've forgot.

TILDEN. It's different for her. She couldn't forget that. How could she forget a thing like that?

DODGE. I don't want to talk about it!

TILDEN. Why'd you tell her it was *your* flesh and blood?

DODGE. I don't want to talk about it.

TILDEN. What do you want to talk about?

DODGE. I don't want to talk about anything! I don't want to talk about troubles or what happened fifty years ago or thirty years ago or the racetrack or Florida or the last time I seeded the corn! I don't want to talk period. Talking just wears me thin.

TILDEN. You don't wanna die do you?

DODGE. No, I don't particularly wanna die either.

TILDEN. Well, you gotta talk or you'll die.

DODGE. Who told you that crap?

TILDEN. That's what I know. I found that out in New Mexico. I thought I was dying but I just lost my voice.

DODGE. Were you with somebody? A woman? A woman'll

22

make you think you're dying, sure as shooting.

TILDEN.   I was alone. I thought I was dead.

DODGE.   Might as well have been. What'd you come back here for?

TILDEN.   I didn't know where else to go.

DODGE.   You're a grown man. You shouldn't be needing your parents at your age. It's unnatural. There's nothing we can do for you now anyway. Couldn't you make a living down there? Couldn't you find some way to make a living? Support yourself? What'dya come back here for? You expect us to feed you forever?

TILDEN.   I didn't know where else to go.

DODGE.   I never went back to my parents. Never. Never even had the urge. I was independent. Always independent. Always found a way. Self-sufficient.

TILDEN.   I didn't know what to do. I couldn't figure anything out.

DODGE.   There's nothing to figure out. You just forge ahead. What's there to figure out? *(Tilden stands.)*

TILDEN.   I was standing. It was night. I was full of the smell of New Mexico. It's different than Illinois. Totally different. Foreign, almost. My lungs were full of it. Like pine smoke and mesquite. That was it. It was foreign. So I left there and I came back here. *(He starts to leave.)*

DODGE.   Where are you going?

TILDEN.   Out back.

DODGE.   You're not suppose to go out there. You heard what she said. Don't play deaf with me!

TILDEN.   I like it out there.

DODGE.   In the rain?

TILDEN.   Especially in the rain. I like the feeling of it. Feels like it always did.

DODGE.   You're supposed to watch out for me. Get me things when I need them.

TILDEN.   What do you need?

DODGE.   I don't need anything yet! But I might. I might need something any second. Any second now. I can't be left alone for a minute! *(Dodge starts to cough.)*

TILDEN. I'll be right outside. You can just yell.

DODGE. *(Between coughs.)* No! It's too far! You can't go out there! It's too far! You might not even hear me! I could die here and you'd never hear me!

TILDEN. *(Moving to pills.)* Why don't you take a pill? You want a pill? *(Dodge coughs more violently, throws himself back against the sofa, clutches his throat. Tilden stands by helplessly.)*

DODGE. Water! Get me some water! *(Tilden rushes off L. Dodge reaches out for the pills, knocking some bottles to the floor, coughing in spasms. He grabs a small bottle, takes out pills and swallows them. Tilden rushes back on with a glass of water. Dodge takes it and drinks, his coughing subsides.)*

TILDEN. You all right now? *(Dodge nods. Drinks more water. Tilden moves in closer to him. Dodge sets glass of water on the night table. His coughing is almost gone.)* Why don't you lay down for a while? Just rest a little. *(Tilden helps Dodge lie down on the sofa. Covers him with blanket.)*

DODGE. You're not going outside are you?

TILDEN. No.

DODGE. I don't want to wake up and find you not here.

TILDEN. I'll be here. *(Tilden tucks blanket around Dodge.)*

DODGE. You'll stay right here?

TILDEN. I'll stay in my chair.

DODGE. That's not a chair. That's my old milking stool.

TILDEN. I know.

DODGE. Don't call it a chair.

TILDEN. I won't. *(Tilden tries to take Dodge's baseball cap off.)*

DODGE. What're you doing! Leave that on me! Don't take that offa me! That's my cap! *(Tilden leaves the cap on Dodge.)*

TILDEN. I know.

DODGE. Bradley'll shave my head if I don't have that on. That's my cap.

TILDEN. I know it is.

DODGE. Don't take my cap off.

TILDEN. I won't.

DODGE. You stay right here now.

TILDEN. *(Sits on stool.)* I will.

DODGE. Don't go outside. There's nothing out there. Never has been. It's empty.

TILDEN. I won't.

DODGE. Everything's in here. Everything you need. Money's on the table. TV. Is the TV on?

TILDEN. Yeah.

DODGE. Turn it off! Turn the damn thing off! What's it doing on?

TILDEN. *(Turns off TV, light goes out.)* You left it on.

DODGE. Well turn it off.

TILDEN. *(Sits on stool again.)* It's off.

DODGE. Leave it off.

TILDEN. I will.

DODGE. When I fall asleep you can turn it back on.

TILDEN. Okay.

DODGE. You can watch the ball game. White Sox. You like the White Sox don't you?

TILDEN. Yeah.

DODGE. You can watch the White Sox. Pee Wee Reese. Pee Wee Reese. You remember Pee Wee Reese?

TILDEN. No.

DODGE. Was he with the White Sox?

TILDEN. I don't know.

DODGE. Pee Wee Reese. *(Falling into sleep.)* Bases loaded. Top a the sixth. Bases loaded. Runner on first and third. Big fat knuckle ball. Floater. Big as a blimp. Cracko! Ball just took off like a rocket. Just pulverized. I marked it. Marked it with my eyes. Straight between the clock and the Burma Shave ad. I was the first kid out there. First kid. I had to fight hard for that ball. I wouldn't give it up. They almost tore the ears right off of me. But I wouldn't give it up. *(Dodge falls into deep sleep. Tilden just sits staring at him for a while. Slowly he leans toward the sofa, checking to see if Dodge is well asleep. He reaches slowly under the cushion and pulls out the bottle of booze. Dodge sleeps soundly. Tilden stands quietly, staring at Dodge as he uncaps the bottle and takes a long drink. He caps the bottle and sticks it in his*

25

hip pocket. He looks around at the husks on the floor and then back to Dodge. He moves C. and gathers an armload of corn husks then crosses back to the sofa. He stands holding the husks over Dodge and looks down at him as he gently spreads the corn husks over the whole length of Dodge's body. He stands back and looks at Dodge. Pulls out bottle, takes another drink, returns bottle to his hip pocket. He gathers more husks and repeats the procedure until the floor is clean of corn husks and Dodge is completely covered in them except for his head. Tilden takes another long drink, stares at Dodge sleeping then quietly exits L. Long pause as the sound of rain continues. Dodge sleeps on.

The figure of Bradley appears U.L., outside the screen porch door. He holds a wet newspaper over his head as a protection from the rain. He seems to be struggling with the door then slips and almost falls to the ground. Dodge sleeps on, undisturbed.)

BRADLEY.   Sonuvabitch! Sonuvagoddamnbitch! Always some obstacle. *(Bradley recovers his footing and makes it through the screen door onto the porch. He throws the newspaper down, shakes the water out of his hair, and brushes the rain off his shoulders. He is a big man dressed in a gray sweatshirt, black suspenders, baggy dark blue pants, and black janitor's shoes. His left leg is wooden, having been amputated above the knee. He moves with an exaggerated, almost mechanical limp. The squeaking sounds of leather accompany his walk coming from the harness and hinges of the false leg. His arms and shoulders are extremely powerful and muscular due to a lifetime of dependency on the upper torso doing all the work for the legs. He is about five years younger than Tilden. He moves laboriously to the R. door and enters, closing the door behind him. He doesn't notice Dodge at first. He moves toward the staircase. Calling upstairs.)* Mom! *(He stops and listens. Turns U. and sees Dodge sleeping. Notices corn husks. He moves slowly toward sofa. Stops next to pail and looks into it. Looks at husks. Dodge stays asleep. Bradley talks to himself.)* Corn. *(Pause.)* Harvest's over, Pops. *(He looks at Dodge's sleeping face and shakes his head in disgust. He pulls out a pair of black electric hair clippers from his pocket. Unwinds the cord and crosses to the lamp. He jabs his wooden leg behind the knee, causing it to bend at the joint and awkwardly kneels to plug the cord into a floor outlet. He pulls himself to his feet again by using the sofa as leverage. He moves to Dodge's head and again jabs his false leg. Goes down on one knee. He violently knocks away some of the corn husks then jerks off Dodge's baseball cap and throws it down C. Dodge stays asleep. Bradley switches on the clippers. Lights start dimming. Bradley cuts Dodge's hair while he sleeps. Lights dim slowly to black with the sound of clippers and rain.)*

ACT TWO

Scene: same set as Act One. Night. Sound of rain. Dodge still asleep on sofa. His hair is cut extremely short and in places the scalp is cut and bleeding. His cap is still center stage. All the corn and husks, pail and milking stool have been cleared away. The lights come up to the sound of a young girl laughing offstage left. Dodge remains asleep. Shelly and Vince appear up left outside the screen porch door sharing the shelter of Vince's overcoat above their heads. Shelly is about nineteen, black hair, very beautiful. She wears tight jeans, high heels, purple T-shirt and a short rabbit fur coat. Her makeup is exaggerated and her hair has been curled. Vince is Tilden's son, about twenty-two, wears a plaid shirt, jeans, dark glasses, cowboy boots and carries a black saxophone case. They shake the rain off themselves as they enter the porch through the screen door.

SHELLY. *(Laughing, gesturing to house.)* This is it? I don't believe this is it!
VINCE. This is it.
SHELLY. This is the house?
VINCE. This is the house.
SHELLY. I don't believe it!
VINCE. How come? It's just a house.
SHELLY. It's like a Norman Rockwell cover or something.
VINCE. What's a matter with that? It's American.
SHELLY. American? Where's the milkman and the little dog? What's the little dog's name? Spot. Spot and Jane. Dick and Jane and Spot. See Spot run.
VINCE. Come on! Knock it off. It's my heritage. *(She laughs more hysterically, out of control.)* Have some respect would ya!
SHELLY. *(Trying to control herself.)* I'm sorry.
VINCE. I don't want to go in there with you acting like an idiot.
SHELLY. Yes sir!

28

VINCE.   Well I don't. I haven't had any contact with them for years. I just don't want them to think I've suddenly arrived out of the middle of nowhere completely deranged.

SHELLY.   What do you want them to think then? *(Pause.)*

VINCE.   Nothing. Let's just go in. *(He crosses porch toward R. interior door. Shelly follows him. He opens the R. door slowly. Vince sticks his head in, doesn't notice Dodge sleeping. Calls out toward staircase.)* Grandma! *(Shelly breaks into laughter, unseen behind Vince. Vince pulls his head back outside and pulls door shut. We hear their voices again without seeing them.)*

SHELLY.   *(Stops laughing.)* I'm sorry. I'm sorry Vince. I really am. I really am sorry. I won't do it again. I couldn't help it.

VINCE.   It's not all that humorous.

SHELLY.   I know it's not. I'm sorry.

VINCE.   I mean this is a tense situation for me! I haven't seen them for over six years. I don't know what to expect.

SHELLY.   I know. I won't do it again. Scout's honor. Just don't say "Grandma," okay? *(She giggles, stops.)* I mean if you say "Grandma," I don't know if I can control myself.

VINCE.   Well try!

SHELLY.   Okay. Sorry. *(He opens the door again. Vince sticks his head in then enters. Shelly follows behind him. Vince crosses to staircase, sets down saxophone case and overcoat, looks up staircase. Shelly notices Dodge's baseball cap. Crosses to it. Picks it up and puts it on her head. Vince goes up the stairs and disappears at the top. Shelly watches him then turns and sees Dodge on the sofa. She takes off the baseball cap.)*

VINCE.   *(From upstairs.)* Grandma! *(From upstairs.)* Grandma! *(Shelly crosses over to Dodge slowly and stands next to him. She stands at his head, reaches out slowly and touches one of the cuts. The second she touches his head, Dodge jerks up to a sitting position on the sofa, eyes open. Shelly gasps. Dodge looks at her, sees his cap in her hands, quickly puts his hand to his bare head. He glares at Shelly then whips the cap out of her hands and puts it on. Shelly backs away from him. Dodge stares at her.)*

SHELLY.   I'm uh — with Vince. *(Dodge just glares at her.)* He's upstairs. *(Dodge looks at the staircase then back at Shelly. Calling upstairs.)* Vince!

VINCE. Just a second!

SHELLY. You better get down here!

VINCE. Just a minute! I'm looking at the pictures. *(Dodge keeps staring at her.)*

SHELLY. *(To Dodge.)* We just got here. We drove out from New York. Pouring rain on the freeway so we thought we'd stop by. I mean Vince was planning on stopping anyway. He wanted to see you. He said he hadn't seen you in a long time. Pay you a little visit. *(Pause. Dodge just keeps staring at her.)* We were going all the way through to New Mexico. To see his father. I guess his father lives out there. In a trailer or something. *(Louder.)* We thought we'd stop by and see you on the way. Kill two birds with one stone, you know? *(She laughs, Dodge stares; she stops laughing.)* I mean Vince has this thing about his family now. I guess it's a new thing with him. I kind of find it hard to relate to. But he feels it's important. You know. I mean he wants to get to know you again. After all this time. Reunite. I don't have much faith in it myself. Reuniting. *(Pause. Dodge just stares at her. She moves nervously to staircase and yells up to Vince.)* Vince will you come down here please! *(Vince comes halfway down the stairs.)*

VINCE. I guess they went out for a while. *(Shelly points to sofa and Dodge. Vince turns and sees Dodge. He comes all the way down staircase and crosses to Dodge. Shelly stays behind, near the staircase, keeping her distance.)* Grandpa? *(Dodge looks up at him, not recognizing him.)*

DODGE. Did you bring the whiskey? *(Vince looks back at Shelly then back to Dodge.)*

VINCE. Grandpa, it's me. Vince. I'm Vince. Tilden's son. You remember? *(Dodge stares at him.)*

DODGE. You didn't do what you told me. You didn't stay here with me.

VINCE. Grandpa, I haven't been here until just now. I just got here.

DODGE. You left. Abandoned me. You went outside like we told you not to do. You went out there in back. In the rain. *(Vince looks back at Shelly. She moves slowly toward the sofa.)*

SHELLY. Is he okay?

VINCE. I don't know. *(Takes off his shades.)* Look, Grandpa, don't you remember me? Vince. Your grandson. I know it's been a while. My hair's longer, maybe. *(Dodge stares at him then takes off his baseball cap.)*

DODGE. *(Points to his head.)* See what happens when you leave me alone? See that? That's what happens. *(Vince looks at Dodge's head, then reaches out to touch it. Dodge slaps Vince's hand away with the cap and puts it back on his head.)*

VINCE. What's going on Grandpa? Where's Halie?

DODGE. Don't worry about her. She won't be back for days. She's absconded. She says she'll be back but she won't be. *(He starts laughing.)* There's life in the old girl yet! *(Stops laughing.)*

VINCE. How did you do that to your head?

DODGE. I didn't do it! Don't be ridiculous! Whadya think I am, an animal?

VINCE. Well who did then? *(Pause. Dodge stares at Vince.)*

DODGE. Who do you think did it? Who do you think? *(Shelly moves toward Vince.)*

SHELLY. Vince, maybe we oughta go. I don't like this. I mean this isn't my idea of a good time.

VINCE. *(To Shelly.)* Just a second. *(To Dodge.)* Grandpa, look, I just got here. I just now got here. I haven't been here for six years. I don't know anything that's happened. *(Pause. Dodge stares at him.)*

DODGE. You don't know anything?

VINCE. No.

DODGE. Well that's good. That's good. It's much better not to know anything. Much, much better.

VINCE. Isn't there anybody here with you? *(Dodge turns slowly and looks off to L.)*

DODGE. Tilden's here.

VINCE. No, Grandpa, Tilden's in New Mexico. That's where I was going. I'm going out there to see him. We just stopped off here because it was on the way. *(Dodge turns slowly back to Vince.)*

DODGE. Well, you're gonna be disappointed. *(Vince backs away and joins Shelly. Dodge stares at them.)*

SHELLY. Vince, why don't we spend the night in a motel

and come back in the morning? We could have breakfast. A shower. Maybe everything would be different.

VINCE.   Don't be scared. There's nothing to be scared of. He's just old.

SHELLY.   I'm not scared!

DODGE.   You two are not my idea of the perfect couple!

SHELLY.   *(After pause.)* Oh really? Why's that?

VINCE.   Shh! Don't aggravate him.

DODGE.   There's something wrong between the two of you. Something not compatible. Like chalk and cheese.

VINCE.   Grandpa, where did Halie go? Maybe we should call her. I don't understand why you're here all by yourself. Isn't anybody looking after you?

DODGE.   What are you talking about? Do you know what you're talking about? Are you just talking for the sake of talking? Lubricating the gums?

VINCE.   I'm just trying to —

DODGE.   Halie is out with her boyfriend. The Right Reverend Dewis. He's not a breeder-man but a man of God. Next best thing I suppose.

VINCE.   I'm trying to figure out what's going on here!

DODGE.   Good luck.

VINCE.   I expected everything to be different. I mean the same. Like it used to be.

DODGE.   Who are you to expect anything? Who are you supposed to be?

VINCE.   I'm Vince! Your grandson! You've gotta remember me.

DODGE.   Vince. My grandson. That's rich!

VINCE.   Tilden's son.

DODGE.   Tilden's son, Vince. He had *two*, I guess.

VINCE.   Two? No look, you haven't seen me for a long time.

DODGE.   When was the last time?

VINCE.   I don't remember exactly. We had a big dinner. A reunion, kind of. Turkey. You made some comment about Dad's fastball. I was a kid, I guess. It was quite a while ago.

DODGE.   You don't remember.

VINCE.   No. Not really. I mean — we were all sitting at the table. All of us — and you and Bradley were making fun of

32

Dad's fastball. And —

DODGE.   You don't remember. How am I supposed to remember if you don't.

VINCE.   I remember being there. I just don't remember the details.

SHELLY.   Vince, come on. This isn't going to work out. I've got a strong feeling.

VINCE.   *(To Shelly.)* Just take it easy.

SHELLY.   I'm taking it easy! He doesn't even know who you are!

VINCE.   *(Crossing to Dodge.)* Of course he knows who I am. He's just tired or something. Grandpa, look — I don't know what's happened here, but —

DODGE.   Stay where you are! Keep your distance! *(Vince stops. Looks back at Shelly then to Dodge.)*

SHELLY.   Vince, this is really making me nervous. I mean he doesn't even want us here. He doesn't even like us.

DODGE.   She's a beautiful girl.

VINCE.   Thanks.

DODGE.   Very "fetching," as they used to say.

SHELLY.   Oh my God.

DODGE.   *(To Shelly.)* What's your name, girlie girl?

SHELLY.   Shelly.

DODGE.   Shelly. That's a man's name isn't it?

SHELLY.   Not in this case.

DODGE.   *(To Vince.)* She's a smart-ass too.

SHELLY.   Vince! Can we go?

VINCE.   Grandpa look — look at me for a second. Try to remember my face.

DODGE.   She wants to go. She just got here and she wants to go. Itchy.

VINCE.   This is kind of strange for her. I mean, it's strange enough for me —

DODGE.   She'll get used to it. *(To Shelly.)* What part of the country do you hail from, girlie?

SHELLY.   Originally?

DODGE.   That's right. Originally. At the very start.

SHELLY.   LA.

33

DODGE.   LA. Stupid country.

SHELLY.   I can't stand this Vince! This is really unbelievable!

DODGE.   It's stupid! LA is stupid! So is Florida. All those Sunshine States. They're all stupid! Do you know why they're stupid?

SHELLY.   Illuminate me.

VINCE.   Shelly. Don't!

DODGE.   I'll tell you why. Because they're full of smart-asses! That's why. *(Shelly turns her back to Dodge, crosses to staircase and sits on bottom step. To Vince.)* Now she's insulted.

SHELLY.   Vince?

DODGE.   She's insulted! Look at her! In my house she's insulted! She's over there sulking because I insulted her!

VINCE.   Grandpa —

SHELLY.   *(To Vince.)* This is really terrific. This is wonderful. And you were worried about me making the right first impression!

DODGE.   *(To Vince.)* She's a fireball isn't she? Regular fireball. I had some a them in my day. Temporary stuff. Never lasted more than a week.

VINCE.   Grandpa — look —

DODGE.   Stop calling me Grandpa will ya! It's sickening. "Grandpa." I'm nobody's grandpa! Least of all yours.

VINCE.   I can't believe you don't recognize me. I just can't believe it. It wasn't that long ago. *(Dodge starts feeling around under the cushion for the bottle of whiskey. Shelly gets up from the staircase.)*

SHELLY.   *(To Vince.)* Maybe you've got the wrong house. Did you ever think of that? Maybe this is the wrong address!

VINCE.   It's not the wrong address! I recognize the yard. The porch. The elm tree. The house. I was standing right here in this house. Right in this very spot.

SHELLY.   Yeah but do you recognize the people? He says he's not your grandfather.

VINCE.   He *is* my grandpa! I know he's my grandpa! He's *always* been my grandpa. He always *will be* my grandpa!

DODGE.   *(Digging for bottle.)* Where's that bottle!

VINCE.   He's just sick or something. I don't know what's happened to him. Delirious.

DODGE. Where's my goddamn bottle! *(Dodge gets up from sofa and starts tearing the cushions off it and throwing them D., looking for the whiskey.)* They've stole my bottle!

SHELLY. Can't we just drive on to New Mexico? This is terrible, Vince! I don't want to stay here. In this house. I thought it was going to be turkey dinners and apple pie and all that kinda stuff.

VINCE. Well I hate to disappoint you!

SHELLY. I'm not disappointed! I'm fuckin' terrified! I wanna go! *(Dodge yells toward L.)*

DODGE. Tilden! Tilden! They stole my bottle! *(Dodge keeps ripping away at the sofa looking for his bottle, he knocks over the nightstand with the bottles. Vince and Shelly watch as he starts ripping the stuffing out of the sofa.)*

VINCE. *(To Shelly.)* He's lost his mind or something. I've got to try to help him.

SHELLY. You help him! I'm leaving! *(Shelly starts to leave. Vince grabs her. They struggle as Dodge keeps ripping away at the sofa and yelling.)*

DODGE. Tilden! Tilden get your ass in here! Tilden!

SHELLY. Let go of me!

VINCE. You're not going anywhere! I need you to stay right here!

SHELLY. Let go of me you sonuvabitch! I'm not your property! *(Suddenly Tilden walks on from L. just as he did before. This time his arms are full of carrots. Dodge, Vince and Shelly stop suddenly when they see him. They all stare at Tilden as he crosses slowly C. with the carrots and stops. Dodge sits on sofa, exhausted.)*

DODGE. *(Panting, to Tilden.)* Where in the hell have you been?

TILDEN. Out back.

DODGE. Where's my bottle?

TILDEN. Gone. *(Tilden and Vince stare at each other. Shelly backs away.)*

DODGE. *(To Tilden.)* You stole my bottle!

VINCE. *(To Tilden.)* Dad? What're you doing here?

SHELLY. Oh brother. *(Tilden just stares at Vince.)*

DODGE. You had no right to steal my bottle! No right at

all! Who do you think you are?

VINCE.   *(To Tilden.)* It's Vince. I'm Vince. *(Tilden stares at Vince then looks at Dodge then turns to Shelly.)*

TILDEN.   *(After pause.)* I picked these carrots. If anybody wants any carrots, I picked 'em.

SHELLY.   *(To Vince.)* Now, wait a minute. This is your father? The one we were going to visit?

VINCE.   *(To Tilden.)* Dad, what're you doing here? What's going on? *(Tilden just stares at Vince, holding carrots, Dodge pulls the blanket back over himself.)*

SHELLY.   This is actually your father? The one in New Mexico?

DODGE.   *(To Tilden.)* You're going to have to get me another bottle! You gotta get me a bottle before Halie comes back! There's money on the table. *(Points to L. kitchen.)*

TILDEN.   *(Shaking his head.)* I'm not going down there. Into town. I never do well in town. *(Shelly crosses to Tilden. Tilden stares at her.)*

SHELLY.   *(To Tilden.)* Are you Vince's father?

TILDEN.   *(To Shelly.)* Vince?

SHELLY.   *(Pointing to Vince.)* This is supposed to be your son! Is he your son? Do you recognize him? I'm just along for the ride here. I thought everybody knew each other! *(Tilden stares at Vince. Dodge wraps himself up in the blanket and sits on sofa staring at the floor.)*

TILDEN.   I had a son once but we buried him. *(Dodge quickly looks at Tilden. Shelly looks to Vince.)*

DODGE.   You shut up about that! You don't know anything about that!

VINCE.   Dad, I thought you were in Bernalillo. We were going to drive down there and see you.

TILDEN.   Long way to drive. Terrible distance.

VINCE.   What's happened, Dad? Has something happened? I thought everything was all right. What's happened to Halie? What're you doing back here?

TILDEN.   She left. Church or something. It's always church. God or Jesus. Or both.

SHELLY.   *(To Tilden.)* Do you want me to take those carrots

36

for you?

VINCE. Shelly — *(Tilden stares at her. She moves in close to him. Holds out her arms. Tilden stares at her arms then slowly dumps the carrots into her arms. Shelly stands there holding the carrots.)*

TILDEN. *(To Shelly.)* You like carrots?

SHELLY. Sure. I like all kinds of vegetables. I'm a vegetarian.

DODGE. *(To Tilden.)* Hitler was a vegetarian. You gotta get me a bottle before Halie comes back! *(Dodge hits sofa with his fist. Vince crosses up to Dodge and tries to console him. Shelly and Tilden stay facing each other.)*

TILDEN. *(To Shelly.)* Backyard's full of carrots. Corn. Potatoes.

SHELLY. You're Vince's father, right? His real father. I'm just asking.

TILDEN. All kinds of vegetables. You like vegetables?

SHELLY. *(Laughs.)* Yeah. I love vegetables.

TILDEN. We could cook these carrots ya know. You could cut 'em up and we could cook 'em. You and me.

SHELLY. All right. Sure. Whatever works.

VINCE. Shelly, what're you doing?

TILDEN. I'll get you a pail and a knife.

SHELLY. Okay.

VINCE. Shelly!

TILDEN. I'll be right back. Don't go.

VINCE. Dad, wait a second. *(Tilden exits off L.)* What the hell is going on here? What's happened to everybody. *(Shelly stands C., arms full of carrots. Vince stands next to Dodge. Shelly looks toward Vince then down at the carrots.)*

DODGE. *(To Vince.)* You could get me a bottle. *(Pointing off L.)* There's money on the table.

VINCE. Grandpa why don't you lay down for a while?

DODGE. I don't wanna lay down for a while! Every time I lay down something happens! *(Whips off his cap, points at his head.)* Look what happens! That's what happens! *(Pulls his cap back on.)* You go lay down and see what happens to you! See how you like it! They'll steal your bottle! They'll cut your hair! They'll murder your children! That's what'll happen. They'll

37

eat you alive.

VINCE.   Just relax for a while. Maybe things will come back to you. *(Pause.)*

DODGE.   You could get me a bottle ya know. There's nothing stopping you from getting me a bottle.

SHELLY.   Why don't you get him a bottle Vince? Maybe it would help everybody identify each other.

DODGE.   *(Pointing to Shelly.)* There, see? She thinks you should get me a bottle. She's a smart cookie. Suddenly, she got smart. *(Vince crosses to Shelly.)*

VINCE.   Shelly, what're you doing with those carrots.

SHELLY.   I'm waiting for your father.

DODGE.   She thinks you should get me a bottle!

VINCE.   Shelly put the carrots down will ya! We gotta deal with the situation here! I'm gonna need your help. I don't know what's going on here but I need some help to try to figure this out.

SHELLY.   I'm helping.

VINCE.   You're only adding to the problem! You're making things worse! Put the carrots down! *(Vince tries to knock the carrots out of her arms. She turns away from him, protecting the carrots.)*

SHELLY.   Get away from me! Stop it! *(Vince stands back from her. She turns to him still holding the carrots.)*

VINCE.   *(To Shelly.)* Why are you doing this? Are you trying to make fun of me? This is my family you know!

SHELLY.   You coulda fooled me! I'd just as soon not be here myself. I'd just as soon be a thousand miles from here. I'd rather be anywhere but here. You're the one who wants to stay. So I'll stay. I'll stay and I'll cut the carrots. And I'll cook the carrots. And I'll do whatever I have to do to survive. Just to make it through this thing.

VINCE.   Put the carrots down Shelly. The carrots aren't going to help. The carrots have nothing to do with the situation here. *(Tilden enters from L. with pail, milking stool, and a knife. He sets the stool and pail C. for Shelly. Shelly looks at Vince then sits down on stool, sets the carrots on the floor and takes the knife from Tilden. She looks at Vince again then picks up a carrot, cuts the ends off, scrapes it and drops it in the pail. She repeats this, Vince glares at her. She smiles.)*

DODGE.   She could get me a bottle. She's the type a girl that could get me a bottle. Easy. She'd go down there. Slink up to the counter. They'd probably give her two bottles for the price of one. She could do that. She has that air about her. *(Shelly laughs. Keeps cutting carrots. Vince crosses up to Dodge, looks at him. Tilden watches Shelly's hands. Long pause.)*

VINCE.   *(To Dodge.)* I haven't changed that much. I mean physically. Physically I'm just about the same. Same size. Same weight. Everything's the same. *(Dodge keeps staring at Shelly while Vince talks to him.)*

DODGE.   She's a beautiful girl. Exceptional. *(Vince moves in front of Dodge to block his view of Shelly. Dodge keeps craning his head around to see her as Vince demonstrates tricks from his past.)*

VINCE.   Look. Look at this. Do you remember this? I used to bend my thumb behind my knuckles. You remember? I used to do it at the dinner table. Way back when. You told me, one day it would get stuck like this and I'd never be able to throw a baseball. *(Vince bends a thumb behind his knuckles for Dodge and holds it out to him. Dodge takes a short glance then looks back at Shelly. Vince shifts position and shows him something else.)* What about this? *(Vince curls his lips back and starts drumming on his teeth with his fingernails making little tapping sounds. Dodge watches a while. Tilden turns toward the sound. Vince keeps it up. He sees Tilden taking notice and crosses to Tilden as he drums on his teeth. Dodge turns TV on and watches it.)* You remember this Dad? Rooty-tooty? "St. James Infirmary"? "When the Saints Go Marching In"? *(Vince keeps on drumming for Tilden. Tilden watches a while, fascinated, then turns back to Shelly. Vince keeps up the drumming on his teeth, crosses back to Dodge doing it. Shelly keeps working on the carrots, talking to Tilden.)*

SHELLY.   *(To Tilden.)* He drives me crazy with that sometimes.

VINCE.   *(To Dodge.)* I know! Here's one you'll remember. You used to kick me out of the house for this one. *(Vince pulls his shirt out of his belt and holds it tucked under his chin with his stomach exposed. He grabs the flesh on either side of his belly button and pushes it in and out to make it look like a mouth talking. He watches his belly button and makes a deep-sounding cartoon voice to synchronize with the movement. He demonstrates it to Dodge then crosses down to Tilden doing it. Both Dodge and Tilden take short, uninterested glances then ignore him. Deep cartoon voice.)* "Hello. How are you? I'm fine. Thank you very much. It's so good to see you looking well this fine Sunday morning." It's the same old me. Same old dependable me. Never change. Never alter one iota. *(Vince stops. Tucks his shirt back in.)*

SHELLY. Vince, don't be pathetic will ya! They're not gonna play. Can't you see that? *(Shelly keeps cutting carrots. Vince slowly moves toward Tilden. Tilden keeps watching Shelly.)*

VINCE. *(To Shelly.)* I don't get it. I really don't get it. Maybe it's me. Maybe I forgot something.

DODGE. *(From sofa.)* You forgot to get me a bottle! That's what you forgot. Anybody in this house could get me a bottle. Anybody! But nobody will. Nobody understands the urgency! Peelin' carrots is more important. Playin' piano on your teeth! Well I hope you all remember this when you get up in years. When you find yourself immobilized. Dependent on the whims of others. *(Vince moves up toward Dodge. Pause as Vince looks at him. Shelly continues cutting carrots. Pause. Vince moves around, stroking his hair, staring at Dodge and Tilden. Vince and Shelly exchange glances. Dodge watches TV.)*

VINCE. Boy! This is amazing. This is truly amazing. *(Keeps moving around.)* What is this anyway? Am I being punished here or what? Is that it? Some kind of banishment? Some kind of wicked warped exile? Just tell me. I can take it. Lay it on me. What was it? Did I betray some secret ancient family taboo, way back when? Did I cross the line somehow when I wasn't looking? What exactly was it?

SHELLY. Vince, what are you doing that for? They don't care about any of that. They just don't recognize you, that's all. They don't have a clue.

VINCE. How could they not recognize me! How in the hell could they not recognize me! I'm their son! I'm their flesh and blood. Anybody can see we're related.

DODGE. *(Watching TV.)* You're no son of mine. I've had sons in my time — plenty of sons but you're not one of 'em. I know them by their scent. *(Long pause. Vince stares at Dodge.)*

VINCE. All right. All right look — I'll get you a bottle. I'll get you a goddamn bottle.

DODGE. You will?

VINCE. Yeah, sure, you bet. If that's what it takes, I'll get you a bottle. Then maybe you can tell me what's going on here.

SHELLY. You're not going to leave me here alone are you?

VINCE. *(Moving to her.)* You suggested it! You said, "Why don't I go get him a bottle." So I'll go get him a bottle! That's what I'll do. Maybe it'll help jar things loose.

SHELLY. But I can't stay here by myself.

DODGE. Don't let her talk you out of it! She's a bad influence. I could see it the minute she stepped in here.

VINCE. Shelly, I gotta go out for a while. I just gotta get outta here. Think things through by myself. I'll get a bottle and I'll come right back.

SHELLY. I don't know if I can handle this Vince.

VINCE. You'll be okay. Nothing's going to happen. They're not dangerous or anything.

SHELLY. Can't we just go?

VINCE. No! I gotta find out what's going on here. Something has fallen apart. This isn't how it used to be. Believe me. This is nothing like how it used to be ...

SHELLY. Look, you think you're bad off, what about me? Not only don't they recognize me but I've never seen them before in my life. I don't know who these guys are. They could be anybody!

VINCE. They're not anybody!

SHELLY. That's what you say.

VINCE. They're my family for Christ's sake! I should know who my own family is! Now give me a break. It won't take that long. I'll just go out and I'll come right back. Nothing'll happen. I promise. *(Shelly stares at him. Pause.)*

SHELLY. Unbelievable.

VINCE. Nothing'll happen. *(He crosses up to Dodge.)* I'm gonna go out now, Grandpa, and I'll pick you up a bottle. Okay?

41

DODGE. Persistence see? That's what it takes. Persistence. Persistence, fortitude and determination. Those are the three virtues. That's how the country was *founded*. You stick with those three and you can't go wrong. *(Pointing off L.)* Money's on the table. In the kitchen. *(Vince moves toward Shelly.)*

VINCE. *(To Shelly.)* You'll be all right, Shelly. I won't be too long.

SHELLY. *(Cutting carrots.)* I'll just keep real busy while you're gone. I love vegetables. *(Vince exits. Tilden keeps staring down at Shelly's hands.)*

VINCE. *(Re-entering, to Tilden.)* You want anything, Dad?

TILDEN. *(Looks up at Vince.)* Me?

VINCE. Yeah, you. "Dad." That's you. From the store? I'm gonna get Grandpa a bottle. Do you want anything from the store?

TILDEN. He's not supposed to drink. Halie wouldn't like it. She'd be disappointed.

VINCE. He wants a bottle.

TILDEN. He's not supposed to drink.

DODGE. *(To Vince.)* Don't negotiate with him! He's the one who stole my bottle! Don't make any transactions until you've spoken to me first! He'll steal you blind!

VINCE. *(To Dodge.)* Tilden says you're not supposed to drink.

DODGE. Tilden's lost his marbles! Look at him! He's around the twist. Take a look at him. He's come unwound. *(Vince stares at Tilden. Tilden watches Shelly's hands as she keeps cutting carrots.)* Now look at me. Look here at me! *(Vince looks back to Dodge.)* Now, between the two of us, who do you think is more trust-worthy? Him or me? Can you trust a man who keeps bring-ing in vegetables from out of nowhere? Take a look at him. *(Vince looks back at Tilden.)*

SHELLY. Go get the bottle Vince. Just go get the bottle.

VINCE. I'll be right back. *(Vince crosses L.)*

DODGE. Where are you going?

VINCE. I'm going to get the money.

DODGE. Then where are you goin'?

VINCE. Liquor store.

DODGE. Don't go off anyplace else. Don't go off some place

and drink by yourself. Come right back here.

VINCE.   I will. *(Vince exits L.)*

DODGE.   *(Calling after Vince.)* You've got responsibility now! And don't go out the back way either! Come out through this way! I wanna see you when you leave! Don't go out the back.

VINCE.   *(Off L.)* I won't! *(Dodge turns and looks at Tilden and Shelly.)*

DODGE.   Untrustworthy. Probably drown himself if he went out the back. Fall right in a hole. I'd never get my bottle.

SHELLY.   I wouldn't worry about Vince. He can take care of himself.

DODGE.   Oh he can, huh? Independent. *(Vince comes on again from L. with two dollars in his hand. He crosses R. past Dodge. To Vince.)* You got the money?

VINCE.   Yeah. Two bucks.

DODGE.   Two bucks. Two bucks is two bucks. Don't sneer.

VINCE.   What kind do you want for two bucks?

DODGE.   Whiskey! Gold Star Sour Mash. Use your own discretion.

VINCE.   Okay.

DODGE.   Nothin' fancy! *(Vince crosses to R. door. Opens it. Stops when he hears Tilden.)*

TILDEN.   *(To Vince.)* You drove all the way from New Mexico?

VINCE.   *(From porch.)* No, I — look — while I'm gone, try to remember who I am. Try real hard to remember. Use your imagination. It might suddenly come back to you. In a flash. *(Vince turns and looks at Tilden. They stare at each other. Vince shakes his head, goes out the door, crosses porch and exits out screen door. Tilden watches him go. Pause.)*

TILDEN.   That's a long, lonely stretch of road. I've driven that stretch before and there's no end to it. You feel like you're going to fall right off into blackness.

SHELLY.   You really don't recognize him? Either one of you? *(Tilden turns again and stares at Shelly's hands as she cuts carrots.)*

DODGE.   *(Watching TV.)* Recognize who?

SHELLY.   Vince.

DODGE.   What's to recognize? *(Dodge lights a cigarette, coughs slightly and stares at TV.)*

SHELLY. It'd be cruel if you recognized him and didn't tell him. Wouldn't be fair.

DODGE. Cruel.

SHELLY. Well it would be. I mean it's not really possible, is it, that he's not related to you at all? Just a stranger? He seems so sure about it. *(Dodge just stares at TV, smoking.)*

TILDEN. I thought I recognized him. I thought I recognized something about him.

SHELLY. You did?

TILDEN. I thought I saw a face inside his face.

SHELLY. Well it was probably that you saw what he used to look like. You haven't seen him for six years.

TILDEN. I haven't?

SHELLY. That's what he says. *(Tilden moves around in front of her as she continues with carrots.)*

TILDEN. Where was it I saw him last?

SHELLY. I have no idea. I've only known him for a few months, myself. He doesn't tell me everything.

TILDEN. He doesn't?

SHELLY. Not stuff like that.

TILDEN. What does he tell you?

SHELLY. You mean in general?

TILDEN. Yeah. *(Tilden moves around behind her.)*

SHELLY. Well he tells me all kinds of things.

TILDEN. Like what?

SHELLY. I don't know! I mean I can't just come out and tell you how he feels.

TILDEN. How come? *(Tilden keeps moving around her slowly in a circle.)*

SHELLY. Because it's stuff he told me privately!

TILDEN. And you can't tell me?

SHELLY. I don't even know you! I'm not even sure *he* knows you.

DODGE. Tilden, go out in the kitchen and make me some coffee! Leave the girl alone. She's nervous. She's ready to jump ship any second.

SHELLY. *(To Dodge.)* He's all right. *(Tilden ignores Dodge, keeps moving around Shelly. He stares at her hair and coat. Dodge stares*

44

at TV.)

TILDEN.   You mean you can't tell me anything?

SHELLY.   I can tell you some things. I mean we can have a conversation.

TILDEN.   We can?

SHELLY.   Sure. We're having a conversation right now.

TILDEN.   We are?

SHELLY.   Yes. That's what we're doing. It's easy.

TILDEN.   But there's certain things you can't tell me, right?

SHELLY.   Right.

TILDEN.   There's certain things I can't tell you either.

SHELLY.   How come?

TILDEN.   I don't know. Nobody's supposed to hear it.

SHELLY.   Well, you can tell me anything you want to.

TILDEN.   I can?

SHELLY.   Sure.

TILDEN.   It might not be very nice.

SHELLY.   That's all right. I've been around.

TILDEN.   It might be awful.

SHELLY.   Well, can't you tell me anything nice? *(Tilden stops in front of her and stares at her coat. Shelly looks back at him. Long pause.)*

TILDEN.   *(After pause.)* Can I touch your coat?

SHELLY.   My coat? *(She looks at her coat then back to Tilden.)* Sure.

TILDEN.   You don't mind?

SHELLY.   No. Go ahead. *(Shelly holds her arm out for Tilden to touch. Dodge stays fixed on TV. Tilden moves in slowly toward Shelly, staring at her arm. He reaches out very slowly and touches her arm, feels the fur gently then draws his hand back. Shelly keeps her arm out.)* It's rabbit.

TILDEN.   Rabbit. *(He reaches out again very slowly and touches the fur on her arm then pulls back his hand again. Shelly drops her arm.)*

SHELLY.   My arm was getting tired.

TILDEN.   Can I hold it? *(Pause.)*

SHELLY.   The coat? Sure. I guess. *(Shelly takes off her coat and*

45

hands it to Tilden. Tilden takes it slowly, feels the fur then puts it on. Shelly watches as Tilden strokes the fur slowly. He smiles at her. She goes back to cutting carrots.) You can have it if you want.

TILDEN. I can?

SHELLY. Yeah. I've got a raincoat in the car. That's all I need.

TILDEN. You've got a car?

SHELLY. Vince does. *(Tilden walks around stroking the fur and smiling at the coat. Shelly watches him when he's not looking. Dodge sticks with TV, stretches out on sofa wrapped in blanket.)*

TILDEN. *(As he walks around.)* I had a car once! I had a white car! I drove. I went everywhere. I went to the mountains. I drove in the snow.

SHELLY. That must've been fun.

TILDEN. *(Still moving, feeling coat.)* I drove all day long sometimes. Across the desert. Way out across the desert. I drove past tiny towns. Anywhere. Past palm trees. Lightning. Anything. I would drive through it. I would drive through it and I would stop and I would look around and I would see things sometimes. I would see things I wasn't supposed to see. Like deer. Hawks. Owls. I would look them in the eye and they would look back and I could tell I wasn't supposed to be there by the way they looked at me. So I'd drive on. I would get back in and drive! I loved to drive. There was nothing I loved more. Nothing I dreamed of was better than driving. I was independent.

DODGE. *(Eyes on TV.)* Pipe down would ya! Stop running off at the mouth. *(Tilden stops. Stares at Shelly.)*

SHELLY. Do you do much driving now?

TILDEN. Now? Now? I don't drive now.

SHELLY. How come?

TILDEN. I'm older.

SHELLY. You're not that old.

TILDEN. I'm not a kid.

SHELLY. You don't have to be a kid to drive.

TILDEN. It wasn't driving then.

SHELLY. What was it?

TILDEN. Adventure. I went everywhere. I had a sensation of myself.

SHELLY. Well you can still do that.

TILDEN. Not now.

SHELLY. Why not?

TILDEN. I just told you. You don't understand. If I told you something you wouldn't understand it.

SHELLY. Told me what?

TILDEN. Told you something that's true.

SHELLY. Like what?

TILDEN. Like a baby. Like a little tiny baby.

SHELLY. Like when you were little?

TILDEN. If I told you you'd make me give your coat back.

SHELLY. I won't. I promise. Tell me. Please.

TILDEN. I can't. Dodge won't let me.

SHELLY. He won't hear you. It's okay. He's watching TV. *(Pause. Tilden stares at her. Moves slightly toward her.)*

TILDEN. We had a baby. Little baby. Could pick it up with one hand. Put it in the other. *(Tilden moves closer to her. Dodge takes more interest.)* So small that nobody could find it. Just disappeared. We had no service. No hymn. Nobody came.

DODGE. Tilden!

TILDEN. Cops looked for it. Neighbors. Nobody could find it. *(Dodge struggles to get up from sofa.)*

DODGE. Tilden? You leave that girl alone! She's completely innocent. *(Dodge keeps struggling until he's standing.)*

TILDEN. Finally everybody just gave up. Just stopped looking. Everybody had a different answer. *(Dodge struggles to walk toward Tilden and falls. Tilden ignores him.)*

DODGE. Tilden! What are you telling her? *(Dodge starts coughing on the floor. Shelly watches him from the stool.)*

TILDEN. Little tiny baby just disappeared. It's not hard. It's so small. Almost invisible. Hold it in one hand. *(Shelly makes a move to help Dodge. Tilden firmly pushes her back down on the stool. Dodge keeps coughing.)*

DODGE. Tilden! Don't tell her anything! She's an outsider!

TILDEN. He's the only one who knows where it is. The only

one. Like a secret buried treasure. Won't tell any of us. *(Dodge's coughing subsides. Shelly stays on stool staring at Dodge. Tilden slowly takes Shelly's coat off and holds it out to her. Long pause. Shelly sits there trembling.)* You probably want your coat back now. I would if I was you. *(Shelly stares at coat but doesn't move to take it. The sound of Bradley's leg squeaking is heard off L. The others onstage remain still. Bradley appears U.L. outside the screen door wearing a yellow rain slicker. He enters through screen door, crosses porch to R. door and enters stage. Closes door. Takes off rain slicker and shakes it out. He sees all the others and stops. Tilden turns to him. Bradley stares at Shelly. Dodge remains on floor.)*

BRADLEY. What's going on here? *(Motioning to Shelly.)* Who's that? *(Shelly stands, moves back away from Bradley as he crosses toward her. He stops next to Tilden. He sees coat in Tilden's hand and grabs it away from him.)* Who's she supposed to be?

TILDEN. She's driving to New Mexico. She has a car. *(Bradley stares at her. Shelly is frozen. Bradley limps over to her with the coat in his fist. He stops in front of her.)*

BRADLEY. *(To Shelly, after pause.)* Vacation? *(Shelly shakes her head "no," trembling. To Shelly, motioning to Tilden.)* You taking him with you? *(Shelly shakes her head "no." Bradley crosses back to Tilden.)* You oughta. No use leaving him here. Doesn't do a lick a work. Doesn't raise a finger. *(Stopping, to Tilden.)* Do ya? *(To Shelly.)* Course he used to be a All-American. Quarterback or fullback or somethin'.

TILDEN. Halfback.

BRADLEY. He tell you about that? Brag on himself? *(Shelly shakes her head "no.")* Yeah, he used to be a big deal. Wore letterman's sweaters. Had medals hanging all around his neck. Real purty. Big damn deal. *(He laughs to himself, notices Dodge on floor, crosses to him, stops.)* This one too. *(To Shelly.)* You'd never think it to look at him, would ya? All paunchy and bloated. *(Shelly shakes her head again. Bradley stares at her, crosses back to her, clenching the coat in his fist. He stops in front of Shelly.)* Women like that kinda thing don't they?

SHELLY. What?

BRADLEY. Importance. Importance in a man.

48

SHELLY. I don't know.

BRADLEY. Yeah. Ya know, ya know. Don't give me that. *(Moves closer to Shelly.)* You're with Tilden?

SHELLY. No.

BRADLEY. *(Turning to Tilden.)* Tilden! She with you? *(Tilden doesn't answer. Stares at floor.)* Tilden! You're gonna run now. Run like a scalded dog! *(Tilden suddenly bolts and runs off U.L. Bradley laughs. Talks to Shelly. Dodge starts moving his lips silently as though talking to someone invisible on the floor. Laughing.)* Scared to death! He was always scared. Scared of his own shadow. *(Bradley stops laughing. Stares at Shelly.)* Some things are like that. They just tremble for no reason. Ever noticed that? They just shake? *(Shelly looks at Dodge on the floor.)*

SHELLY. Can't we do something for him?

BRADLEY. *(Looking at Dodge.)* We could shoot him. *(Laughs.)* Put him out of his misery.

SHELLY. Shut up! *(Bradley stops laughing. Moves in closer to Shelly. She freezes. Bradley speaks slowly and deliberately.)*

BRADLEY. Hey! Missus. Don't talk to me like that. Don't talk to me in that tone a voice. There was a time when I had to take that tone a voice from pretty near everyone. *(Motioning to Dodge.)* Him, for one! When he was a whole man. Full of himself. Him and that half-brain that just ran outa here. They don't talk to me like that now. Not anymore. Everything's turned around now. Full circle. Isn't that funny?

SHELLY. I'm sorry.

BRADLEY. Open your mouth.

SHELLY. What?

BRADLEY. *(Motioning for her to open her mouth.)* Open up. *(She opens her mouth slightly.)* Wider. *(She opens her mouth wider.)* Keep it like that. *(She does. Stares at Bradley. With his free hand he puts his fingers into her mouth. She tries to pull away.)* Just stay put! *(She freezes. He keeps his fingers in her mouth. Stares at her. Pause. He pulls his hand out. She closes her mouth, keeps her eyes on him. Bradley smiles. He looks at Dodge on the floor and crosses over to him. Shelly watches him closely. Bradley stands over Dodge and smiles at Shelly. He holds her coat up in both hands over Dodge, keeps smil-*

ing at Shelly. He looks down at Dodge then drops the coat so that it lands on Dodge and covers his head. Bradley keeps his hands up in the position of holding the coat, looks over at Shelly and smiles. The lights black out.)

ACT THREE

Scene: same set. Morning. Bright sun. No sound of rain. Everything has been cleared up again. No sign of carrots. No pail. No stool. Vince's saxophone case and overcoat are still at the foot of the staircase. Bradley is asleep on the sofa under Dodge's blanket, his head toward stage left. Bradley's wooden leg is leaning against the sofa right by his head. The shoe is left on. The harness hangs down. Dodge is sitting on the floor, propped up against the TV set facing stage left, wearing his baseball cap. Shelly's rabbit fur coat covers his chest and shoulders. He stares toward stage left. He seems weaker and more disoriented. The lights rise slowly to the sound of birds. The two men remain for a while in silence. Bradley sleeps very soundly. Dodge hardly moves. Shelly appears from stage left with a big smile, slowly crossing toward Dodge balancing a steaming cup of broth in a saucer. Dodge just stares at her as she gets close to him.

SHELLY.   (*As she crosses.*) This is going to make all the difference in the world, Grandpa. You don't mind me calling you Grandpa do you? I mean I know you minded when Vince called you that but you don't even know him.

DODGE.   I'm nobody's Grandpa. He skipped town with my money you know. I'm gonna hold you as collateral.

SHELLY.   He'll be back. Don't you worry. He always comes back.

DODGE.   The faithful type.

SHELLY.   No. Determined. (*She kneels down next to Dodge and puts the cup and saucer in his lap.*)

DODGE.   It's morning already! When did it get to be morning? Not only didn't I get my bottle but he's got my two bucks! I'm surrounded by thieves.

SHELLY.   Try to drink this, okay? Don't spill it.

DODGE.   What is it?

SHELLY.   Beef bouillon. It'll warm you up.

51

DODGE. Bouillon! I don't want any goddamn bouillon! Get that stuff away from me!

SHELLY. I just got through making it.

DODGE. I don't care if you just spent all week making it! I ain't drinking it!

SHELLY. Well, what am I supposed to do with it? I'm trying to help you out. Besides, it's good for you.

DODGE. Get it away from me! *(Shelly stands up with cup and saucer.)* What do you know what's good for me anyway? *(She looks at Dodge then turns away from him, crosses to staircase, sits on bottom step and drinks the bouillon. Dodge stares at her.)* You know what'd be good for me?

SHELLY. What?

DODGE. A little backrub. A little contact.

SHELLY. Oh no. I've had enough contact for a while. Thanks anyway. *(She keeps sipping the bouillon, stays sitting. Pause as Dodge stares at her.)*

DODGE. Why not? You got nothing better to do. That fella's not gonna be back here. You're not expecting him to show up again are you?

SHELLY. Sure. He'll show up. He left his horn here.

DODGE. His horn? *(Laughs.)* You're his horn?

SHELLY. Very funny.

DODGE. He's run off with my money! That's what he did. He's not coming back here.

SHELLY. He'll be back. This is where he's from. He knows that. He's convinced. And so am I.

DODGE. You're a funny chicken, you know that?

SHELLY. Funny?

DODGE. Full of hope. Faith. Faith and hope. You're all alike you hopers. If it's not God then it's a man. If it's not a man then it's a woman. If it's not a woman then it's politics or bee pollen or the future of some kind. Some kind of future.

SHELLY. Bee pollen?

DODGE. Yeah, bee pollen. *(Pause.)*

SHELLY. *(Looking toward porch.)* I'm glad it stopped raining. *(Dodge looks toward porch then back to Shelly.)*

DODGE. That's what I mean. See, you're glad it stopped

raining. Now you think everything's gonna be different. Just 'cause the sun comes out.

SHELLY.   It's already different. Last night I was scared.

DODGE.   Scared a what?

SHELLY.   Just scared.

DODGE.   Yeah, well we've all got an instinct for disaster. We can smell it coming.

SHELLY.   It was your son. Bradley. He scared me.

DODGE.   Bradley? *(Looks at Bradley.)* He's a push-over. 'Specially now. All ya gotta do is take his leg and throw it out the back door. Helpless. Totally helpless. *(Shelly turns and stares at Bradley's wooden leg then looks at Dodge. She sips bouillon.)*

SHELLY.   You'd do that?

DODGE.   Me? I've hardly got the strength to breathe.

SHELLY.   But you'd actually do it if you could?

DODGE.   Don't be so easily shocked, girlie. There's nothing a man can't do. You dream it up and he can do it. Anything. It boggles the imagination.

SHELLY.   You've tried I guess.

DODGE.   Don't sit there sippin' your bouillon and judging me! This is my house!

SHELLY.   I forgot.

DODGE.   You forgot? Whose house did you think it was?

SHELLY.   Mine. *(Dodge just stares at her. Long pause. She sips from cup.)* I know it's not mine but I had that feeling.

DODGE.   What feeling?

SHELLY.   The feeling that nobody lives here but me. I mean everybody's gone. You're here, but it doesn't seem like you're supposed to be. *(Pointing to Bradley.)* Doesn't seem like he's supposed to be here either. I don't know what it is. It's the house or something. Something familiar. Like I know my way around here. Did you ever get that feeling? *(Dodge stares at her in silence. Pause.)*

DODGE.   No. No, I never did. I get lost in the hallway sometimes. *(Shelly gets up. Moves around space holding cup.)*

SHELLY.   Last night I went to sleep up there in that room.

DODGE.   What room?

SHELLY.   That room up there with all the pictures. All the

53

crosses on the wall.

DODGE. Halie's room?

SHELLY. Yeah. Whoever "Halie" is.

DODGE. She's my wife.

SHELLY. So you remember her?

DODGE. Whadya mean! 'Course I remember her. She's only been gone a day — half a day. However long it's been.

SHELLY. Do you remember her when her hair was bright red? Standing in front of an apple tree?

DODGE. What is this, the third degree or something! Who're you to be askin' me personal questions about my wife!

SHELLY. You never look at those pictures up there?

DODGE. What pictures!

SHELLY. Your whole life's up there hanging on the wall. Somebody who looks just like you. Somebody who looks just like you used to look.

DODGE. That isn't me! That never was me! This is me. Right here. This is it. The whole shootin' match, sittin' right here in front of you. That other stuff was a sham.

SHELLY. So the past never happened as far as you're concerned?

DODGE. The past? Jesus Christ. The past is passed. What do you know about the past?

SHELLY. Not much. I know there was a farm. *(Pause.)*

DODGE. A farm?

SHELLY. There's a picture of a farm. A big farm. A bull. Wheat. Corn.

DODGE. Corn?

SHELLY. All the kids are standing out in the corn. They're all waving these big straw hats. One of them doesn't have a hat.

DODGE. Which one was that?

SHELLY. There's a baby. A baby in a woman's arms. The same woman with the red hair. She looks lost standing out there. Like she doesn't know how she got there.

DODGE. She knows! I told her a hundred times it wasn't gonna be the city! I gave her plenty a warning.

SHELLY. She's looking down at the baby like it was somebody else's. Like it didn't even belong to her.

DODGE.   That's about enough outta you! You got some funny ideas, sister. Some damn funny ideas. You think just because people propagate they have to love their offspring? You never seen a bitch eat her puppies? Where are you from anyway?

SHELLY.   LA. We already went through that.

DODGE.   That's right, LA I remember.

SHELLY.   Stupid country.

DODGE.   That's right! No wonder. Dumber than dirt. *(Pause.)*

SHELLY.   What's happened to this family anyway?

DODGE.   You're in no position to ask! What do you care? You some kinda social worker?

SHELLY.   I'm Vince's friend.

DODGE.   Vince's friend! That's rich. That's real rich. "Vince"! "Mr. Vince"! "Mr. Thief" is more like it! His name doesn't mean a hoot in hell to me. Not a tinkle in the well. You know how many kids I've spawned? Not to mention grandkids and great-grandkids and great-great-grandkids after them?

SHELLY.   And you don't remember any of them?

DODGE.   What's to remember? Halie's the one with the family album. She's the one you should talk to. She'll set you straight on the heritage if that's what you're interested in. She's traced it all the way back to the grave.

SHELLY.   What do you mean?

DODGE.   What do you think I mean? How far back can you go? A long line of corpses! There's not a living soul behind me. Not a one. Who gives a damn about bones in the ground?

SHELLY.   What was Tilden trying to tell me last night? *(Dodge stops short. Stares at Shelly. Shakes his head. He looks off L. Dodge's tone changes drastically.)*

DODGE.   Tilden? *(Turns to Shelly, calmly.)* Where is Tilden?

SHELLY.   What was he trying to say about the baby? *(Pause. Dodge turns toward L.)*

DODGE.   What's happened to Tilden? Why isn't Tilden here?

SHELLY.   Bradley chased him out.

DODGE.   *(Looking at Bradley asleep.)* Bradley? Why is he on my sofa? *(Turns back to Shelly.)* Have I been here all night? On

55

the floor?

SHELLY.　　He wouldn't leave. I hid outside until he fell asleep.

DODGE.　　Outside? Is Tilden outside? He shouldn't be out there in the rain. He'll get himself into trouble. He doesn't know his way around here anymore. Not like he used to. He went out West and got himself into trouble. Deep trouble. We don't want any of that around here.

SHELLY.　　What did he do? *(Pause.)*

DODGE.　　*(Quietly stares at Shelly.)* Tilden? He got mixed up. That's what he did. We can't afford to leave him alone. Not now. *(Sound of Halie laughing comes from off L. Shelly stands, looking in direction of voice, holding cup and saucer, doesn't know whether to stay or run. Motioning to Shelly.)* Sit down! Sit back down! *(Shelly sits. Sound of Halie's laughter again. To Shelly in a heavy whisper, pulling coat up around him.)* Don't leave me alone now! Promise me? Don't go off and leave me alone. I need somebody here with me. Tilden's gone now and I need someone. Don't leave me! Promise!

SHELLY.　　*(Sitting.)* I won't. *(Halie appears outside the screen porch door, U.L. with Father Dewis. She is wearing a bright yellow dress, no hat, white gloves and her arms are full of yellow roses. Father Dewis is dressed in traditional black suit, white clerical collar and shirt. He is a very distinguished gray-haired man in his sixties. They are both slightly drunk and feeling giddy. As they enter the porch through the screen door, Dodge pulls the rabbit fur coat over his head and hides. Shelly stands again. Dodge drops the coat and whispers intently to Shelly. Neither Halie nor Father Dewis are aware of the people inside the house.)*

DODGE.　　*(To Shelly in a strong whisper.)* You promised! *(Shelly sits on stairs again. Dodge pulls coat back over head. Halie and Father Dewis talk on the porch as they cross toward R. interior door.)*

HALIE.　　Oh Father! That's terrible! That's absolutely terrible! Aren't you afraid of being punished? *(She giggles.)*

DEWIS.　　Not by the Italians. They're too busy punishing each other. *(They both break out in giggles.)*

HALIE.　　What about God?

DEWIS.　　Well, prayerfully, God only hears what he wants to.

That's just between you and me of course. In our heart of hearts we know we're every bit as wicked as the Catholics. *(They giggle again and reach the R. door.)*

HALIE.   Father, I never heard you talk like this in Sunday sermon.

DEWIS.   Well, I save all my best jokes for private company. Pearls before swine you know. *(They enter the room laughing and stop when they see Shelly. Shelly stands. Halie closes the door behind Father Dewis. Dodge's voice is heard under the coat talking to Shelly.)*

DODGE.   *(Under coat, to Shelly.)* Sit down, sit down! Don't let 'em buffalo you. *(Shelly sits on stair again. Halie looks at Dodge on the floor, then looks at Bradley asleep on the sofa and sees his wooden leg. She lets out a shriek of embarrassment for Father Dewis.)*

HALIE.   Oh my gracious! What in the name of Judas Priest is going on in this house! *(She hands over the roses to Father Dewis.)* Excuse me Father. *(Halie crosses to Dodge, whips the coat off him and covers the wooden leg with it. Bradley stays asleep.)* You can't leave this house for a second without the devil blowing in the front door!

DODGE.   Gimme back that coat! Gimme back that goddamn coat before I freeze to death!

HALIE.   You're not going to freeze! The sun's out in case you hadn't noticed!

DODGE.   Gimme back that coat! That coat's for live flesh not dead wood. *(Halie whips the blanket off Bradley and throws it on Dodge. Dodge covers his head again with blanket. Bradley's amputated leg can be faked by having it under a cushion on the sofa. Bradley's fully clothed. He sits up with a jerk when the blanket comes off him.)*

HALIE.   *(As she tosses blanket.)* Here! Use this! It's yours anyway! Can't you take care of yourself for once!

BRADLEY.   *(Yelling at Halie.)* Gimme that blanket! Gimme back that blanket! That's my blanket! *(Halie crosses back toward Father Dewis who just stands there with the roses. Bradley thrashes helplessly on the sofa trying to reach the blanket. Dodge hides himself deeper in the blanket. Shelly looks on from staircase, still holding cup and saucer.)*

HALIE.   Believe me, Father, this is not what I had in mind

57

when I invited you in. I keep forgetting how easily things fall
to pieces when I'm not here to hold them together.

DEWIS.   Oh, no apologies please. I wouldn't be in the min-
istry if I couldn't face real life. *(Father Dewis laughs self-con-
sciously. Halie notices Shelly again and crosses over to her. Shelly stays
sitting. Halie stops and stares at her.)*

BRADLEY.   I want my blanket back! Gimme my blanket!
(Halie turns toward Bradley and silences him.)

HALIE.   Shut up Bradley! Right this minute. I've had enough!
It's shameful the way you carry on. *(Bradley slowly recoils, lies
back down on sofa, turns his back toward Halie and whimpers softly.
Halie directs her attention to Shelly again. Pause.)*

BRADLEY.   You gave me that blanket.

HALIE.   Enough. *(To Shelly.)* What are you doing with my
cup and saucer?

SHELLY.   *(Looking at cup, back to Halie.)* I made some bouillon for Dodge.

HALIE.   For Dodge?

SHELLY.   Yeah.

HALIE.   My husband, Dodge.

SHELLY.   Yes.

HALIE.   You're here in my house making bouillon for my
husband.

SHELLY.   Yes.

HALIE.   Well, did he drink it?

SHELLY.   No.

HALIE.   Did you drink it?

SHELLY.   Yes. *(Halie stares at her. Long pause. She turns abruptly
away from Shelly and crosses back to Father Dewis.)*

HALIE.   Father, there's a stranger in my house. What would
you advise? What would be the Christian thing?

DEWIS.   *(Squirming.)* Oh, well ... I ... I really — is she a tres-
passer?

HALIE.   We still have some whiskey, don't we? A drop or
two? *(Dodge slowly pulls the blanket down and looks toward Father
Dewis. Shelly stands.*

SHELLY.   Listen, I don't drink or anything. I just — *(Halie
turns toward Shelly viciously.)*

HALIE.   You sit back down! *(Shelly sits again on stair. Halie turns again to Dewis.)* I think we still have plenty of whiskey left! Don't we Father?

DEWIS.   Well, yes. I think so. You'll have to get it. My hands are full. *(Halie giggles. Reaches into Dewis's pockets, searching for bottle. She smells the roses as she searches. Dewis stands stiffly. Dodge watches Halie closely as she looks for bottle.)*

HALIE.   Roses. The most incredible things, roses! Aren't they incredible, Father?

DEWIS.   Yes. Yes they are.

HALIE.   They almost cover the stench of sin in this house. Hanky-panky. Just magnificent! The smell. We'll have to put some at the foot of Ansel's statue. On the day of the unveiling. *(Halie finds a silver flask of whiskey in Dewis's vest pocket. She pulls it out. Dodge looks on eagerly. Halie crosses to Dodge, opens the flask and takes a sip. To Dodge.)* Ansel's getting a statue, Dodge. Did you know that? Not a plaque but a real live statue. A full bronze. Tip to toe. A basketball in one hand and a rifle in the other.

BRADLEY.   *(His back to Halie.)* He never played basketball!

HALIE.   You better shut up, Bradley! You shut up about Ansel! Ansel played basketball better than anyone! And you know it! He was an All-American! There's no reason to take the glory away from others. Especially when one's own shortcomings are so apparent. *(Halie turns away from Bradley, crosses back toward Dewis sipping on the flask and smiling. To Dewis.)* Ansel was a great basketball player. Make no mistake. One of the greatest.

DEWIS.   I remember Ansel. Handsome lad. Tall and strapping.

HALIE.   Of course! You remember. You remember how he could play. *(She turns toward Shelly.)* Of course, nowadays they play a different brand of basketball. More vicious. Isn't that right, dear?

SHELLY.   I don't know. *(Halie crosses to Shelly, sipping on flask. She stops in front of Shelly.)*

HALIE.   Much, much more vicious. They smash into each other. They knock each other's teeth out. There's blood all over the court. Savages. Barbaric, don't you think? *(Halie takes the cup from Shelly and pours whiskey into it.)* They don't train like they used to. Not at all. They allow themselves to run amuck. Drugs and women. Women mostly. *(Halie hands the cup of whiskey back to Shelly slowly. Shelly takes it.)* Mostly women. Girls. Sad, pathetic little skinny girls. *(She crosses back to Father Dewis.)* It's just a reflection of the times, don't you think Father? An indication of where we stand?

DEWIS.   I suppose so, yes. I've been so busy with the choir —

HALIE.   Yes. A sort of bad omen. Our youth becoming monsters.

DEWIS.   Well, I uh — wouldn't go quite that far.

HALIE.   Oh you can disagree with me if you want to, Father. I'm open to debate. *(She moves toward Dodge.)* I suppose, in the long run, it doesn't matter. When you see the way things deteriorate before your very eyes. Everything running down hill. It's kind of silly to even think about youth.

DEWIS.   No, I don't think so. I think it's important to believe in certain things. Certain basic truths. I mean —

HALIE.   Yes. Yes, I know what you mean. I think that's right. I think that's true. *(She looks at Dodge.)* Certain basic things. We can't shake the fundamentals. We might end up crazy. Like my husband. You can see it in his eyes. You can see the madness almost oozing out. *(Dodge covers his head with the blanket again. Halie takes a single rose from Dewis and moves slowly over to Dodge.)* We can't not believe in something. We can't stop believing. We just end up dying if we stop. Just end up dead. *(Halie throws the rose gently onto Dodge's blanket. It lands between his knees and stays there. Long pause as Halie stares at the rose.)*

BRADLEY.   Ansel never played basketball.

HALIE.   Bradley, I'm warning you. *(Shelly stands suddenly. Halie doesn't turn to her but keeps staring at the rose.)*

SHELLY.   *(To Halie.)* Don't you wanna know who I am? Don't you wanna know what I'm doing here! Standing in the middle of your house. I'm not dead! *(Shelly crosses toward Halie. Halie turns slowly to her.)*

HALIE.   Did you drink your whiskey?

SHELLY. No! And I'm not going to either!

HALIE. Well that's a firm stand. It's good to have a firm stand.

SHELLY. I don't have any stand at all. I'm just trying to put all this together. *(Halie laughs and crosses back to Dewis.)*

HALIE. *(To Dewis.)* Surprises, surprises! Did you have any idea we'd be returning to this?

DEWIS. Well, actually —

SHELLY. I came here with your grandson for a little visit! A little innocent friendly visit.

HALIE. My grandson?

SHELLY. Yes! That's right. The one no one seems to remember.

HALIE. *(To Dewis.)* This is getting a little far-fetched.

SHELLY. I told him it was stupid to come back here. To try to pick up from where he left off.

HALIE. Where was that?

SHELLY. Wherever he was when he left here! Six years ago! Ten years ago! Whenever it was! I told him nobody cares. I told him nobody cares anymore. Nobody's going to care.

HALIE. Didn't he listen?

SHELLY. No! No he didn't. We had to stop off at every tiny little meatball town that he remembered from his boyhood!

HALIE. My grandson?

SHELLY. Every dumb little donut shop he ever kissed a girl in. Every drive-in. Every drag strip. Every football field he ever broke a bone on.

HALIE. *(Suddenly alarmed, to Dodge.)* Where's Tilden?

SHELLY. Don't ignore me! I'm telling you something!

HALIE. Dodge! Where's Tilden gone? *(Shelly moves violently toward Halie.)*

SHELLY. *(To Halie.)* I'm talking to you! I'm standing here talking to you. *(Bradley sits up fast on the sofa, Shelly backs away.)*

BRADLEY. *(To Shelly.)* Don't you yell at my mother!

HALIE. Dodge! *(She kicks Dodge.)* I told you not to let Tilden out of your sight! Where's he gone to?

DODGE. Gimme a drink and I'll tell ya.

DEWIS. Halie, maybe this isn't the right time for a visit.

(Halie crosses back to Dewis.)

HALIE. *(To Dewis.)* I never should've left! I never, never should've left! Tilden could be anywhere now! Anywhere! He's not in control of his faculties. He wanders. You know how he wanders. Dodge knew that. I told him when I left here. I told him specifically to watch out for Tilden. *(Bradley reaches down, grabs Dodge's blanket and yanks it off him. He lays down on the sofa and pulls the blanket over his head.)*

DODGE. He's got my blanket again! He's got my blanket!

HALIE. *(Turning to Bradley.)* Bradley! Bradley, put that blanket back! *(Halie moves toward Bradley. Shelly suddenly throws the cup and saucer against the R. door. Dewis ducks. The cup and saucer smash into pieces. Halie stops, turns toward Shelly. Everyone freezes. Bradley slowly pulls his head out from under blanket, looks toward R. door, then to Shelly. Shelly stares at Halie. Dewis cowers with roses. Shelly moves slowly toward Halie. Long pause. Shelly speaks softly.)*

SHELLY. *(To Halie.)* I am here! I am standing right here in front of you. I am breathing. I am speaking. I am alive! I exist. *DO YOU SEE ME?*

BRADLEY. *(Sitting up on sofa.)* We don't have to tell you anything, girl. Not a thing. You're not the police are you? You're not the government. You're just some prostitute that Tilden brought in here.

HALIE. Language! I won't have that language in my house! Father I'm —

SHELLY. *(To Bradley.)* You stuck your hand in my mouth and you call me a prostitute! What kind of a weird fucked-up yo-yo are you?

HALIE. Bradley! Did you put your hand in this girl's mouth? You have no idea what kind of diseases she might be carrying.

BRADLEY. I never did. She's lying. She's lying through her teeth.

DEWIS. Halie, I think I'll be running along now. I'll just put the roses in the kitchen. Keep them fresh. A little sugar sometimes helps. *(Dewis moves toward L. Halie stops him.)*

HALIE. Don't go now, Father! Not now. Please — I'm not

sure I can stay afloat.

BRADLEY. I never did anything, Mom! I never touched her! She propositioned me! And I turned her down. I turned her down flat! She's not my type. You know that Mom. *(Shelly suddenly grabs her coat off the wooden leg and takes both the leg and coat D., away from Bradley.)* Mom! Mom! She's got my leg! She's taken my leg! I never did anything to her! She's stolen my leg! She's a devil Mom. How did she get in our house? *(Bradley reaches pathetically in the air for his leg. Shelly sets it down for a second, puts on her coat fast and picks up the leg again. Dodge starts coughing again softly.)*

HALIE. *(To Shelly.)* I think we've had about enough of you young lady. Just about enough. I don't know where you came from or what you're doing here but you're no longer welcome in this house.

SHELLY. *(Laughs, holds leg.)* No longer welcome!

BRADLEY. Mom! That's my leg! Get my leg back! I can't do anything without my leg! She's trying to torture me. *(Bradley keeps on making whimpering sounds and reaching for his leg.)*

HALIE. Give my son back his leg. Right this very minute! Dodge, where did this girl come from? *(Dodge starts laughing softly to himself in between coughs.)*

DODGE. She's a pistol, isn't she?

HALIE. *(To Dewis.)* Father, do something about this would you! I'm not about to be terrorized in my own house!

DEWIS. This is out of my domain.

BRADLEY. Gimme back my leg!

HALIE. Oh, shut up Bradley! Just shut up! You don't need your leg now! Just lay down and shut up! I've never heard such whining. *(Bradley whimpers, lies down and pulls blanket around him. He keeps one arm outside blanket, reaching out toward his wooden leg. Dewis cautiously approaches Shelly with the roses in his arms. Shelly clutches the wooden leg to her chest as though she's kidnapped it.)*

DEWIS. *(To Shelly.)* Now, honestly, dear, wouldn't it be better to talk things out? To try to use some reason? No point in going off the deep end. Nothing to be gained in that.

SHELLY. There isn't any reason here! I can't find a reason

for anything.

DEWIS.   There's nothing to be afraid of. These are all good people. All righteous souls.

SHELLY.   I'm not afraid!

DEWIS.   But this is not your house. You have to have some respect.

SHELLY.   You're the strangers here, not me.

HALIE.   This has gone on far enough!

DEWIS.   Halie, please. Let me handle this. I've had some experience.

SHELLY.   Don't come near me! Don't anyone come near me. I don't need any words from you. I'm not threatening anybody. I don't even know what I'm doing here. You all say you don't remember Vince, okay, maybe you don't. Maybe it's Vince that's crazy. Maybe he's made this whole family thing up. I don't even care anymore. I was just coming along for the ride. I thought it'd be a nice gesture. Besides, I was curious. He made all of you sound familiar to me. Every one of you. For every name, I had an image. Every time he'd tell me a name, I'd see the person. In fact, each of you was so clear in my mind that I actually believed it was you. I really believed that when I walked through that door that the people who lived here would turn out to be the same people in my imagination. Real people. People with faces. But I don't recognize any of you. Not one. Not even the slightest resemblance.

DEWIS.   Well you can hardly blame others for not fulfilling your hallucination.

SHELLY.   It was no hallucination! It was more like a prophecy. You believe in prophecy, don't you, Father?

HALIE.   Father, there's no point in talking to her any further. We're just going to have to call the police.

BRADLEY.   No! Don't get the police in here. We don't want the police in here. This is our home.

SHELLY.   That's right. Bradley's right. Don't you usually settle your affairs in private? Don't you usually take them out in the dark? Out in the back?

BRADLEY.   You stay out of our lives! You have no business interfering!

SHELLY.   I don't have any business period. I got nothing to lose. I'm a free agent. *(She moves around, staring at each of them.)*
BRADLEY.   You don't know what we've been through. You don't know anything about us!
SHELLY.   I know you've got a secret. You've all got a secret. It's so secret, in fact, you're all convinced it never happened. *(Halie moves to Dewis.)*
HALIE.   Oh, my God, Father! Who is this person?
DODGE.   *(Laughing to himself.)* She thinks she's going to get it out of us. She thinks she's going to uncover the truth of the matter. Like a detective or something.
BRADLEY.   I'm not telling her anything! Nothing's wrong here! Nothing's ever been wrong! Everything's the way it's supposed to be! Nothing ever happened that's bad. Everything is all right here! We're all good people! We've always been good people. Right from the very start.
DODGE.   She thinks she's gonna suddenly bring everything out into the open after all these years.
DEWIS.   *(To Shelly.)* Can't you see that these people want to be left in peace? Don't you have any mercy? They haven't done anything to you.
DODGE.   She wants to get to the bottom of it. *(To Shelly.)* That's it, isn't it? You'd like to get right down to bedrock? Look the beast right dead in the eye. You want me to tell ya? You want me to tell ya what happened? I'll tell ya. I might as well. I wouldn't mind hearing it hit the air after all these years of silence.
BRADLEY.   No! Don't listen to him. He doesn't remember anything!
DODGE.   I remember the whole thing from start to finish. I remember the day he was born. *(Pause.)*
HALIE.   Dodge, if you tell this thing — if you tell this, you'll be dead to me. You'll be just as good as dead.
DODGE.   That won't be such a big change, Halie. See this girl, this little girl here, she wants to know. She wants to know something more. And I got this feeling that it doesn't make a bit a difference. I'd sooner tell it to a stranger than anybody else. I'd sooner tell it to the four winds.

65

BRADLEY. *(To Dodge.)* We made a pact! We made a pact between us! You can't break that now!

DODGE. I don't remember any pact. *(Silence.)* See, we were a well-established family once. Well-established. All the boys were grown. The farm was producing enough milk to fill Lake Michigan twice over. Me and Halie here were pointed toward what looked like the middle part of our life. Everything was settled with us. All we had to do was ride it out. Then Halie got pregnant again. Out the middle a nowhere, she got pregnant. We weren't planning on havin' any more boys. We had enough boys already. In fact, we hadn't been sleepin' in the same bed for about six years.

HALIE. *(Moving toward stairs.)* I'm not listening to this! I don't have to listen to this!

DODGE. *(Stops Halie.)* Where are you going! Upstairs! You'll just be listenin' to it upstairs! You go outside, you'll be listenin' to it outside. Might as well stay here and listen to it. *(Halie stays by stairs. Pause.)* Halie had this kid see. This baby boy. She had it. I let her have it on her own. All the other boys I had had the best doctors, the best nurses, everything. This one I let her have by herself. This one hurt real bad. Almost killed her, but she had it anyway. It lived, see. It lived. It wanted to grow up in this family. It wanted to be just like us. It wanted to be part of us. It wanted to pretend that I was its father. She wanted me to believe in it. Even when everyone around us knew. Everyone. All our boys knew. Tilden knew.

HALIE. You shut up! Bradley, make him stop!

BRADLEY. I can't.

DODGE. Tilden was the one who knew. Better than any of us. He'd walk for miles with that kid in his arms. Halie let him take it. All night sometimes. He'd walk all night out there in the pasture with it. Talkin' to it. Singin' to it. Used to hear him singing to it. He'd make up stories. He'd tell that kid all kinds a stories. Even when he knew it couldn't understand him. We couldn't let a thing like that continue. We couldn't allow that to grow up right in the middle of our lives. It made everything we'd accomplished look like it was nothin'. Everything was canceled out by this one mistake. This one weakness.

SHELLY. So you ...

DODGE. I killed it. I drowned it. Just like the runt of a litter. Just drowned it. There was no struggle. No noise. Life just left it. *(Halie moves toward Bradley.)*

HALIE. *(To Bradley.)* Ansel would've stopped him! Ansel would've stopped him from telling these lies! He was a hero! A man! A whole man! What's happened to the men in this family! Where are the men! *(Suddenly Vince comes crashing through the screen porch door U.L., tearing it off its hinges. Everyone but Dodge and Bradley back away from the porch and stare at Vince, who has landed on his stomach on the porch in a drunken stupor. He is singing loudly to himself and hauls himself slowly to his feet. He has a paper shopping bag full of empty booze bottles. He takes them out one at a time as he sings and smashes them at the opposite end of the porch, behind the solid interior door, R. Shelly moves slowly toward R., holding wooden leg and watching Vince.)*

VINCE. *(Singing loudly as he hurls bottles.)* "From the halls of Montezuma to the shores of Tripoli. We will fight our country's battles in the air on land and sea." *(He punctuates the words "Montezuma," "Tripoli," "battles," and "sea" with a smashed bottle each. He stops throwing for a second, stares toward R. of the porch, shades his eyes with his hand as though looking across to a battlefield, then cups his hands around his mouth and yells across the space of the porch to an imaginary army. The others watch in terror and expectation. To imagined army.)* Have you had enough over there! 'Cause there's a lot more here where that came from! *(Pointing to paper bag full of bottles.)* A helluva lot more! We got enough over here to blow ya from here to Kingdom come! *(He takes another bottle, makes high whistling sound of a bomb and throws it toward R. porch. Sound of bottle smashing against wall. This should be the actual smashing of bottle and not tape sound. He keeps yelling and heaving bottles one after another. Vince stops for a while, breathing heavily from exhaustion. Long silence as the others watch him. Shelly approaches tentatively in Vince's direction, still holding Bradley's wooden leg.)*

SHELLY. *(After silence.)* Vince? *(Vince turns toward her. Peers through screen.)*

VINCE. Who? What? Vince who? Who's that in there? Is someone in there? *(Vince pushes his face against the screen from the porch and stares in at everyone.)*

DODGE. Where's my goddamn bottle!

VINCE. *(Looking in at Dodge.)* What? Who is that? Who's speaking. Who's voice is that?

DODGE. It's me! Your grandfather! Don't play stupid with me! Where's my two bucks!

VINCE. Grandfather? Grandfather? You mean the father of my father? The son of my great-grandfather? That one? When did this start?

DODGE. Where's my bottle! *(Halie moves away from Dewis, U., peers out at Vince, trying to recognize him.)*

HALIE. Vincent? Is that you, Vincent? *(Shelly stares at Halie then looks out at Vince.)*

VINCE. *(From porch.)* Vincent who? What is this! Who are you people?

SHELLY. *(To Halie.)* Hey, wait a minute. Wait a minute!

HALIE. *(Moving closer to porch screen.)* We thought you were a murderer or something. Barging in through the door like that.

VINCE. A murderer? No, no, no! How could I be a murderer when I don't exist? A murderer is a living breathing person who takes the life and breath away from another living breathing person. That's a murderer. You've got me mixed up with someone else.

BRADLEY. *(Sitting up on sofa.)* You get off our front porch you creep! What're you doing out there breaking bottles? Who are these foreigners anyway! Where did they all come from?

HALIE. *(Moving toward porch.)* Vincent, what's got into you! Why are you acting like this?

VINCE. Who's that? Who's that speaking?

SHELLY. *(Approaching Halie.)* You mean you know who he is?

HALIE. Of course I know who he is! That's more than I can say for you missie.

DODGE. Where's my goddamn bottle? *(Halie turns back toward Dewis and crosses to him. Vince sings.)*

VINCE. "From the halls of Montezuma to the shores of Tripoli. We will fight our country's battles in the air on land and sea ..."

HALIE. *(To Dewis.)* Father, why are you just standing around here when everything's falling apart? Can't you rectify this situation? *(Dodge laughs, coughs.)*

DEWIS. I'm just a guest here, Halie. I don't know what my position is exactly. This is outside my parish anyway. I'm in the quiet part of town.

SHELLY. Vince! Knock it off will ya! I want to get out of here! This is enough.

VINCE. *(To Shelly.)* Have they got you prisoner in there, dear? *(Vince starts starts to sing again, throwing more bottles as things continue.)*

SHELLY. I'm coming out there, Vince! I'm coming out there and I want us to get in the car and drive away from here. Anywhere. Just away from here. Far, far away. *(Shelly moves toward Vince's saxophone case and overcoat. She sets down the wooden leg D.L. and picks up the saxophone case and overcoat. Vince watches her through the screen. Shelly moves to R. door and opens it.)*

VINCE. We'd never make it. We'd drive and we'd drive and we'd drive and we'd never make it. We'd think we were getting farther and farther away. That's what we'd think.

SHELLY. I'm coming out there now, Vince.

VINCE. Don't come out. Don't you dare come out here. It's off limits. Taboo territory. *(Vince pulls out a big folding hunting knife and pulls open the blade. He jabs the blade into the screen and starts cutting a hole big enough to climb through. Bradley cowers in a corner of the sofa as Vince rips open the screen. Dewis takes Halie by the arm and pulls her toward staircase.)*

DEWIS. Halie, maybe we should go upstairs until this blows over. I'm completely at a loss.

HALIE. I don't understand it. I just don't understand it. He was the sweetest little boy! There was no indication. *(Dewis drops the roses beside the wooden leg at the foot of the staircase then escorts Halie quickly up the stairs. Halie keeps looking back at Vince as they climb the stairs.)* There wasn't a mean bone in his body. Everybody loved Vincent. Everyone. He was the perfect baby. So pink and perfect.

DEWIS. He'll be all right after a while. He's just had a few too many that's all.

HALIE. He used to sing in his sleep. He'd sing. In the middle of the night. The sweetest voice. Like an angel. *(She stops for a moment.)* I used to lie awake listening to it. I used to lie awake thinking it was all right if I died. Because Vincent was an angel. A guardian angel. He'd watch over us. He'd watch over all of us. He would see to it that no harm would come. *(Dewis takes her all the way up the stairs. They disappear above. Vince is now climbing through the porch screen onto the sofa. Bradley crashes off the sofa, holding tight to his blanket, keeping it wrapped around him. Shelly is outside on the porch. Vince holds the knife in his teeth once he gets the hole wide enough to climb through. Bradley starts crawling slowly toward his wooden leg, reaching out for it.)*

DODGE. *(To Vince.)* Go ahead! Take over the house! Take over the whole goddamn house! You can have it! It's yours! It's been a pain in the neck ever since the very first mortgage. I'm gonna die any second now. Any second. You won't even notice. So I'll settle my affairs once and for all. *(As Dodge proclaims his last will and testament, Vince climbs into the room, knife in mouth and strides slowly around the space, inspecting his inheritance. He casually notices Bradley as he crawls toward his leg. Vince moves to the leg and keeps pushing it with his foot so that it's out of Bradley's reach then goes on with his inspection. He picks up the roses and carries them around smelling them. Shelly can be seen outside on the porch, moving slowly C. and staring in at Vince. Vince ignores her.)* The house goes to my grandson, Vincent. That's fair and square. All the furnishings, accoutrements and paraphernalia therein. Everything tacked to the walls or otherwise resting under this roof. My tools — namely my band saw, my skill saw, my drill press, my chain saw, my lathe, my electric sander all go to my eldest son, Tilden. That is, if he ever shows up again. My Benny Goodman records, my harnesses, my bits, my halters, my brace, my rough rasp, my forge, my welding equipment, my shoeing nails, my levels and bevels, my milking stool — no, not my milking stool — my hammers and chisels and all related materials are to be pushed into a gigantic heap and set ablaze in the very center of my fields. When the blaze is at its highest, preferably on a cold, windless night, my body is to be pitched into the middle of it and burned 'til nothing remains but ash. *(Pause. Vince takes the knife out of his mouth and smells the roses. He's facing toward audience and doesn't turn around to Shelly. He folds up knife and pockets it.)*

SHELLY. *(From porch.)* I'm leaving, Vince. Whether you come or not, I'm leaving. I can't stay here.

VINCE. *(Smelling roses.)* You'll never make it. You'll see.

SHELLY. *(Moving toward hole in screen.)* You're not coming? *(Vince stays D., turns and looks at her.)*

VINCE. I just inherited a house. I've finally been recognized. Didn't you hear?

SHELLY. *(Through hole, from porch.)* You want to stay here?

VINCE. *(As he pushes Bradley's leg out of reach.)* I've gotta carry on the line. It's in the blood. I've gotta see to it that things keep rolling. *(Bradley looks up at him from floor, keeps pulling himself toward his leg. Vince keeps moving it.)*

SHELLY. What happened to you, Vince? You just disappeared. *(Pause. Vince delivers the following speech front.)*

VINCE. I was gonna run last night. I was gonna run and keep right on running. Clear to the Iowa border. I drove all night with the windows open. The old man's two bucks flapping right on the seat beside me. It never stopped raining the whole time. Never stopped once. I could see myself in the windshield. My face. My eyes. I studied my face. Studied everything about it as though I was looking at another man. As though I could see his whole race behind him. Like a mummy's face. I saw him dead and alive at the same time. In the same breath. In the windshield I watched him breathe as though he was frozen in time and every breath marked him. Marked him forever without him knowing. And then his face changed. His face became his father's face. Same bones. Same eyes. Same nose. Same breath. And his father's face changed to his grandfather's face. And it went on like that. Changing. Clear on back to faces I'd never seen before but still recognized. Still recognized the bones underneath. Same eyes. Same mouth. Same breath. I followed my family clear into Iowa. Every last one. Straight into the corn belt and further. Straight back as far as they'd take me. Then it all dissolved. Everything dissolved. Just like that. And that two bucks kept right on flapping on the seat beside me. *(Shelly stares at him for a while then reaches through the hole in the screen and sets the saxophone case and Vince's overcoat on the sofa. She looks at Vince again.)*

SHELLY. Bye Vince. I can't hang around for this. I'm not even related. *(She exits L. off the porch. Vince watches her go. Bradley tries to make a lunge for his wooden leg. Vince quickly picks it up and dangles it over Bradley's head like a carrot. Bradley keeps making desperate grabs at the leg. Dewis comes down the staircase and stops halfway, staring at Vince and Bradley. Vince looks up at Dewis and smiles. He keeps moving backwards with the leg toward U.L. as Bradley crawls after him.)*

VINCE. *(To Dewis as he continues torturing Bradley.)* Oh, excuse me, Father. Just getting rid of some of the vermin in the house. This is my house now, ya know? All mine. Everything. Except for the power tools and stuff. I'm gonna get all new equipment anyway. New plows, new tractor, everything. All brand-new. *(Vince teases Bradley closer to the U.L. corner of the stage.)* Start right off on the ground floor. *(Vince throws Bradley's wooden leg far offstage L. Bradley follows his leg offstage, pulling himself along on the ground, whimpering. As Bradley exits, Vince pulls the blanket off him and throws it over his own shoulder. He crosses toward Dewis with the blanket and smells the roses. Dewis comes to the bottom of the stairs.)*

DEWIS. You'd better go up and see your grandmother. I think you should. It would be the Christian thing.

VINCE. *(Looking upstairs, back to Dewis.)* My grandmother? There's nobody else in this house. Except for you. And you're leaving aren't you? *(Dewis crosses toward R. door. He turns back to Vince.)*

DEWIS. She's going to need someone. I can't help her. I don't know what to do. I don't know what my position is here. I'm quite out of my depths. I'll be the first to admit it. I thought, by now, the Lord would have given me some sign, some guidepost, but I haven't seen it. No sign at all. Just — *(Vince just stares at him. Dewis goes out the door, crosses porch and exits L. Vince listens to him leaving. He smells roses, looks up the staircase then smells roses again. He turns and looks U. at Dodge. He crosses up to him and bends over, looking at Dodge's open eyes. Dodge is dead. His death should have come completely unnoticed. Vince lifts the blanket, then covers Dodge's head. He puts Dodge's cap on his own head and smells the roses while staring at Dodge's body. Long pause. Vince places the roses on Dodge's chest then lays down on the sofa, arms folded behind his head, staring at the ceiling, his body in the same position as Dodge's. After a while, Halie is heard coming from above the staircase. The lights start to dim imperceptively as Halie speaks. Vince keeps staring at the ceiling.)*

HALIE'S VOICE. Dodge? Is that you Dodge? Tilden was right about the corn you know. I've never seen such corn. Have you taken a look at it lately? Dazzling. Tall as a man already. This early in the year. Carrots too. Potatoes. Peas. It's like a paradise out there, Dodge. You oughta take a look. A miracle. I've never seen it like this. Maybe the rain did something. Maybe it was the rain. *(As Halie keeps talking offstage, Tilden appears from L., dripping with mud from the knees down. His arms and hands are covered with mud. In his hands he carries the corpse of a small child at chest level, staring down at it. The corpse mainly consists of bones wrapped in muddy, rotten cloth. He moves slowly D. toward the staircase ignoring Vince on the sofa. Vince keeps staring at the ceiling as though Tilden wasn't there. As Halie continues, Tilden slowly makes his way up the stairs. His eyes never leave the corpse of the child. The lights keep fading.)* Good hard rain. Takes everything straight down deep to the roots. The rest takes care of itself. You can't force a thing to grow. You can't interfere with it. It's all hidden. Unseen. You just gotta wait 'til it pops up out of the ground. Tiny little shoot. Tiny little white shoot. All hairy and fragile. Strong though. Strong enough to crack the earth even. It's a miracle, Dodge. I've never seen a crop like this in my whole life. Maybe it's the sun. Maybe that's it. Maybe it's the sun. *(Tilden disappears above. Silence. Lights go to black.)*

END OF PLAY

PROPERTY LIST

Umbrella (HALIE)
Bottle of whiskey (DODGE)
Old, brown blanket (DODGE)
Pack of cigarettes (DODGE)
Lighter or matches (DODGE)
Bunch of fresh corn (TILDEN)
Chewing tobacco (TILDEN)
Milking stool (TILDEN)
Pail (TILDEN)
Spittoon (TILDEN)
Elbow-length gloves (HALIE)
Bottles of pills (HALIE, DODGE)
Glass of water (TILDEN)
Baseball cap (DODGE)
Wet newspaper (BRADLEY)
Black, electric hair clippers, with cord (BRADLEY)
Overcoat (VINCE)
Black saxophone case (VINCE)
Sunglasses (VINCE)
Bunch of carrots (TILDEN)
Knife (TILDEN)
2 one-dollar bills (VINCE)
Rabbit fur coat (SHELLY)
Wooden leg (BRADLEY)
Cup and saucer with broth (SHELLY)
Bouquet of yellow roses (HALIE)
Silver flask of whiskey (FATHER DEWIS)
Paper bag of empty booze bottles (VINCE)
Corpse of child, wrapped in muddy, rotten cloth (TILDEN)

SOUND EFFECTS

Light rain
Birds

NEW PLAYS

★ **THE EXONERATED by Jessica Blank and Erik Jensen.** Six interwoven stories paint a picture of an American criminal justice system gone horribly wrong and six brave souls who persevered to survive it. "The #1 play of the year...intense and deeply affecting..." –*NY Times.* "Riveting. Simple, honest storytelling that demands reflection." –*A.P.* "Artful and moving...pays tribute to the resilience of human hearts and minds." –*Variety.* "Stark...riveting...cunningly orchestrated." –*The New Yorker.* "Hard-hitting, powerful, and socially relevant." –*Hollywood Reporter.* [7M, 3W] ISBN: 0-8222-1946-8

★ **STRING FEVER by Jacquelyn Reingold.** Lily juggles the big issues: turning forty, artificial insemination and the elusive scientific Theory of Everything in this Off-Broadway comedy hit. "Applies the elusive rules of string theory to the conundrums of one woman's love life. Think *Sex and the City* meets *Copenhagen.*" –*NY Times.* "A funny offbeat and touching look at relationships...an appealing romantic comedy populated by oddball characters." –*NY Daily News.* "Where kooky, zany, and madcap meet...whimsically winsome." –*NY Magazine.* "STRING FEVER will have audience members happily stringing along." –*TheaterMania.com.* "Reingold's language is surprising, inventive, and unique." –*nytheatre.com.* "...[a] whimsical comic voice." –*Time Out.* [3M, 3W (doubling)] ISBN: 0-8222-1952-2

★ **DEBBIE DOES DALLAS adapted by Erica Schmidt, composed by Andrew Sherman, conceived by Susan L. Schwartz.** A modern morality tale told as a comic musical of tragic proportions as the classic film is brought to the stage. "A scream! A saucy, tongue-in-cheek romp." –*The New Yorker.* "Hilarious! DEBBIE manages to have it all: beauty, brains and a great sense of humor!" –*Time Out.* "Shamelessly silly, shrewdly self-aware and proud of being naughty. Great fun!" –*NY Times.* "Racy and raucous, a lighthearted, fast-paced thoroughly engaging and hilarious send-up." –*NY Daily News.* [3M, 5W] ISBN: 0-8222-1955-7

★ **THE MYSTERY PLAYS by Roberto Aguirre-Sacasa.** Two interrelated one acts, loosely based on the tradition of the medieval mystery plays. "... stylish, spine-tingling...Mr. Aguirre-Sacasa uses standard tricks of horror stories, borrowing liberally from masters like Kafka, Lovecraft, Hitchcock...But his mastery of the genre is his own...irresistible." –*NY Times.* "Undaunted by the special-effects limitations of theatre, playwright and *Marvel* comic-book writer Roberto Aguirre-Sacasa maps out some creepy twilight zones in THE MYSTERY PLAYS, an engaging, related pair of one acts...The theatre may rarely deliver shocks equivalent to, say, *Dawn of the Dead,* but Aguirre-Sacasa's work is fine compensation." –*Time Out.* [4M, 2W] ISBN: 0-8222-2038-5

★ **THE JOURNALS OF MIHAIL SEBASTIAN by David Auburn.** This epic one-man play spans eight tumultuous years and opens a uniquely personal window on the Romanian Holocaust and the Second World War. "Powerful." –*NY Times.* "[THE JOURNALS OF MIHAIL SEBASTIAN] allows us to glimpse the idiosyncratic effects of that awful history on one intelligent, pragmatic, recognizably real man..." –*NY Newsday.* [3M, 5W] ISBN: 0-8222-2006-7

★ **LIVING OUT by Lisa Loomer.** The story of the complicated relationship between a Salvadoran nanny and the Anglo lawyer she works for. "A stellar new play. Searingly funny." –*The New Yorker.* "Both generous and merciless, equally enjoyable and disturbing." –*NY Newsday.* "A bitingly funny new comedy. The plight of working mothers is explored from two pointedly contrasting perspectives in this sympathetic, sensitive new play." –*Variety.* [2M, 6W] ISBN: 0-8222-1994-8

DRAMATISTS PLAY SERVICE, INC.
440 Park Avenue South, New York, NY 10016 212-683-8960 Fax 212-213-1539
postmaster@dramatists.com www.dramatists.com

NEW PLAYS

★ **MATCH by Stephen Belber.** Mike and Lisa Davis interview a dancer and choreographer about his life, but it is soon evident that their agenda will either ruin or inspire them—and definitely change their lives forever. "Prolific laughs and ear-to-ear smiles." *–NY Magazine.* "Uproariously funny, deeply moving, enthralling theater. Stephen Belber's MATCH has great beauty and tenderness, and abounds in wit." *–NY Daily News.* "Three and a half out of four stars." *–USA Today.* "A theatrical steeplechase that leads straight from outrageous bitchery to unadorned, heartfelt emotion." *–Wall Street Journal.* [2M, 1W] ISBN: 0-8222-2020-2

★ **HANK WILLIAMS: LOST HIGHWAY by Randal Myler and Mark Harelik.** The story of the beloved and volatile country-music legend Hank Williams, featuring twenty-five of his most unforgettable songs. "[LOST HIGHWAY has] the exhilarating feeling of Williams on stage in a particular place on a particular night...serves up classic country with the edges raw and the energy hot...By the end of the play, you've traveled on a profound emotional journey: LOST HIGHWAY transports its audience and communicates the inspiring message of the beauty and richness of Williams' songs...forceful, clear-eyed, moving, impressive." *–Rolling Stone.* "...honors a very particular musical talent with care and energy... smart, sweet, poignant." *–NY Times.* [7M, 3W] ISBN: 0-8222-1985-9

★ **THE STORY by Tracey Scott Wilson.** An ambitious black newspaper reporter goes against her editor to investigate a murder and finds the *best* story...but at what cost? "A singular new voice...deeply emotional, deeply intellectual, and deeply musical..." *–The New Yorker.* "...a conscientious and absorbing new drama..." *–NY Times.* "...a riveting, tough-minded drama about race, reporting and the truth..." *–A.P.* "... a stylish, attention-holding script that ends on a chilling note that will leave viewers with much to talk about." *–Curtain Up.* [2M, 7W (doubling, flexible casting)] ISBN: 0-8222-1998-0

★ **OUR LADY OF 121st STREET by Stephen Adly Guirgis.** The body of Sister Rose, beloved Harlem nun, has been stolen, reuniting a group of life-challenged childhood friends who square off as they wait for her return. "A scorching and dark new comedy... Mr. Guirgis has one of the finest imaginations for dialogue to come along in years." *–NY Times.* "Stephen Guirgis may be the best playwright in America under forty." *–NY Magazine.* [8M, 4W] ISBN: 0-8222-1965-4

★ **HOLLYWOOD ARMS by Carrie Hamilton and Carol Burnett.** The coming-of-age story of a dreamer who manages to escape her bleak life and follow her romantic ambitions to stardom. Based on Carol Burnett's bestselling autobiography, *One More Time.* "...pure theatre and pure entertainment..." *–Talkin' Broadway.* "...a warm, fuzzy evening of theatre." *–BrodwayBeat.com.* "...chuckles and smiles of recognition or surprise flow naturally...a remarkable slice of life." *–TheatreScene.net.* [5M, 5W, 1 girl] ISBN: 0-8222-1959-X

★ **INVENTING VAN GOGH by Steven Dietz.** A haunting and hallucinatory drama about the making of art, the obsession to create and the fine line that separates truth from myth. "Like a van Gogh painting, Dietz's story is a gorgeous example of excess—one that remakes reality with broad, well-chosen brush strokes. At evening's end, we're left with the author's resounding opinions on art and artifice, and provoked by his constant query into which is greater: van Gogh's art or his violent myth." *–Phoenix New Times.* "Dietz's writing is never simple. It is always brilliant. Shaded, compressed, direct, lucid—he frames his subject with a remarkable understanding of painting as a physical experience." *–Tucson Citizen.* [4M, 1W] ISBN: 0-8222-1954-9

DRAMATISTS PLAY SERVICE, INC.
440 Park Avenue South, New York, NY 10016 212-683-8960 Fax 212-213-1539
postmaster@dramatists.com www.dramatists.com

NEW PLAYS

★ **INTIMATE APPAREL by Lynn Nottage.** The moving and lyrical story of a turn-of-the-century black seamstress whose gifted hands and sewing machine are the tools she uses to fashion her dreams from the whole cloth of her life's experiences. "...Nottage's play has a delicacy and eloquence that seem absolutely right for the time she is depicting..." –*NY Daily News.* "...thoughtful, affecting...The play offers poignant commentary on an era when the cut and color of one's dress—and of course, skin—determined whom one could and could not marry, sleep with, even talk to in public." –*Variety.* [2M, 4W] ISBN: 0-8222-2009-1

★ **BROOKLYN BOY by Donald Margulies.** A witty and insightful look at what happens to a writer when his novel hits the bestseller list. "The characters are beautifully drawn, the dialogue sparkles..." –*nytheatre.com.* "Few playwrights have the mastery to smartly investigate so much through a laugh-out-loud comedy that combines the vintage subject matter of successful writer-returning-to-ethnic-roots with the familiar mid-life crisis." –*Show Business Weekly.* [4M, 3W] ISBN: 0-8222-2074-1

★ **CROWNS by Regina Taylor.** Hats become a springboard for an exploration of black history and identity in this celebratory musical play. "Taylor pulls off a Hat Trick: She scores thrice, turning CROWNS into an artful amalgamation of oral history, fashion show, and musical theater..." –*TheatreMania.com.* "...wholly theatrical...Ms. Taylor has created a show that seems to arise out of spontaneous combustion, as if a bevy of department-store customers simultaneously decided to stage a revival meeting in the changing room." –*NY Times.* [1M, 6W (2 musicians)] ISBN: 0-8222-1963-8

★ **EXITS AND ENTRANCES by Athol Fugard.** The story of a relationship between a young playwright on the threshold of his career and an aging actor who has reached the end of his. "[Fugard] can say more with a single line than most playwrights convey in an entire script...Paraphrasing the title, it's safe to say this drama, making its memorable entrance into our consciousness, is unlikely to exit as long as a theater exists for exceptional work." –*Variety.* "A thought-provoking, elegant and engrossing new play..." –*Hollywood Reporter.* [2M] ISBN: 0-8222-2041-5

★ **BUG by Tracy Letts.** A thriller featuring a pair of star-crossed lovers in an Oklahoma City motel facing a bug invasion, paranoia, conspiracy theories and twisted psychological motives. "...obscenely exciting...top-flight craftsmanship. Buckle up and brace yourself..." –*NY Times.* "...[a] thoroughly outrageous and thoroughly entertaining play...the possibility of enemies, real and imagined, to squash has never been more theatrical." –*A.P.* [3M, 2W] ISBN: 0-8222-2016-4

★ **THOM PAIN (BASED ON NOTHING) by Will Eno.** An ordinary man muses on childhood, yearning, disappointment and loss, as he draws the audience into his last-ditch plea for empathy and enlightenment. "It's one of those treasured nights in the theater—treasured nights anywhere, for that matter—that can leave you both breathless with exhilaration and...in a puddle of tears." –*NY Times.* "Eno's words...are familiar, but proffered in a way that is constantly contradictory to our expectations. Beckett is certainly among his literary ancestors." –*nytheatre.com.* [1M] ISBN: 0-8222-2076-X

★ **THE LONG CHRISTMAS RIDE HOME by Paula Vogel.** Past, present and future collide on a snowy Christmas Eve for a troubled family of five. "...[a] lovely and hauntingly original family drama...a work that breathes so much life into the theater." –*Time Out.* "...[a] delicate visual feast..." –*NY Times.* "...brutal and lovely...the overall effect is magical." –*NY Newsday.* [3M, 3W] ISBN: 0-8222-2003-2

DRAMATISTS PLAY SERVICE, INC.
440 Park Avenue South, New York, NY 10016 212-683-8960 Fax 212-213-1539
postmaster@dramatists.com   www.dramatists.com